A Ticket to Eternity

A return journey

Javier Gonzalez

A Ticket to Eternity©
November 15th 2014
Javier Gonzalez
ISBN: 1503359913
Edition and design: Jose Diaz Diaz
Cover and Layout: Nelson Diaz

All rights reserved. This publication may not be reproduced, in whole or in part, or recorded or transmitted by a retrieval system in any form or by any means, mechanical, photo-mechanical, electronic, magnetic, electro-optical, photocopying or otherwise, without the prior written permission of the author.

Collection: "The Cavern, School of Creative Writing"

Dedication

I am thinking about you my reader friend, I would like you to be attracted by that white light too, that you may also experience that peace, tranquillity and love of the eternal life. Our existence has several chapters, we are "in transit" in our mother's womb, we are also transiting through our earthly, material life, another chapter of our existence is the eternal life.

We much enjoy the chapter of our earthly life, despite it's sad moments and it's rewards, we all live differently and nobody has a perfect life. We try to walk and we manage that, we have access to food, drink, to the air that we breathe and we give thanks for what we have, what we manage to obtain and share. We choose the destiny of our own soul, the ticket that we have in our own hands, could be to go to the so called Heaven or to the so called Hell, they both exist, I have visited them and came back to tell you about them.

I remember so many people that were here, alive and are now deceased, others that are still here, enjoying , suffering , dreaming , thinking , for those wondering , why me ?, why ?, what has happened ... ?

I 'm still being selfish and do not want you to fall into the eternal suffering, I would like you to get ready to see the eternal light, to you I dedicate this book.

The day which we fear as our last is but the birthday of eternity.
Seneca *(2 AC-65) Roman Philosopher*

Prologue

In February 1975, an underground train failed to stop at Moorgate Station, in the City of London and crashed against a concrete wall, 30 meters below ground. The train was travelling at 40mph (60Km/h) and 43 passengers died in horrific circumstances in the front coach, the rescue workers had to go through even more crude experiences. I survived from the first carriage. When the accident happened, I was injured and received a blow in my head, that left me unconscious, I had a NDE (Near death Experience), arriving in "heaven", full of "that white light" and then in I arrived in "hell", that dark place, hot and full of screams, only to come back when I heard a voice shouting "is there anybody else there!?" My life changed, although not immediately.

Through the years I have been through several profound and unexplainable experiences, like getting DVT (Deep Vein Thrombosis) on both legs and PE (Pulmonary Embolism), being in intensive care in the hospital and a few months later, I was not just fully recovered, but did not show signs of having being so seriously ill. I have developed unusual "intuition", for example "hearing" a phone before it rings and originating "remote" messages through an "apparition" of a person.

My wife is also a survivor of cancer, twice and together we have had more strange and unusual experiences. Recently, a friend asked me to write a book, which I have just completed, with the title "A ticket to Eternity – a return journey", where I describe many of these events and some of the conclusions I have arrived at, all true facts. One of the thoughts relates to the date we are born and the date when we will die, these are the dates of our existence in our human body, our "life" (existence) continues in different forms. The "chapter" of our existence, before we are born, is when we exist in our mother's womb, then we are "born", when we leave her body and eventually, something similar happens when our body dies and our "soul" is "born", as it leaves our body and goes into the "chapter" of eternity. A mother makes sure her baby is born in good health, to give it the best opportunity in life and similarly, we are responsible to give the best opportunity to our soul, when it goes into eternal life. Just like the mother took care in preparing her baby, it is our obligation to take sufficient care, interest and dedication to feed our soul, before it is "born", to give it the best chance in "life" in the eternal light and not send it to the eternal darkness.

All material elements during the time we are in use of our bodies tend to distract us from the true meaning of our existence. We are so "absorbed" by all the material aspects of the "body" chapter in our life, that we are "tempted" to generate our "idols" (god-like) objects which we "desire", cars, chocolates, phones, dresses...money...and we tend to lose sight of the facts that in the two "chapters" of our life, contiguous to the "body" chapter, none of these material things are relevant there. The chapter before our body-life (before we are born) takes place inside our mother's womb and the chapter after our body-life (when our body dies), is when our "soul" leaves our body to enter the eternal life.

I went "up" towards that white light, in that peaceful and loving place and then, I went "down" to the dark and hot one, this would seem to indicate that it is possible to move from one place to the other, although I was not "consciously" driving my soul in either direction, I was simply "floating" in each direction. When we are in our mother's womb, we not only receive the love and care of our mothers, but we also receive the "good" (and sometimes "bad") vibrations of others around her. Our soul may also be "pushed-up" by the prayers or "good intentions" of those that remain in the "body" state of life.

Introduction

Accidents, strange events are usually those that happen to other people, not to yourself, however, if they happen to you? Surely then you would believe that these rare happenings can be real. Having the winning ticket to the lottery, or surviving a train crash, an avalanche or receiving unusual messages would make you different, but to go through life with a number of these situations would make you wonder why? Visiting heaven and hell is possible, telling those real life stories, is more difficult and understanding the messages takes time, not everyone gets a chance to have these experiences.

If you heard someone shout "Is there anybody else there???!!!" would you answer? I actually heard that call. Without knowing why, I answered that call, deep down in an obscure tunnel, surrounded by bodies of dead and mutilated bodies. I had just been to a place full of white light, peaceful, attractive...and also to the other place, dark, hot and full of screams...This was the scene of an underground train that had failed to stop at the final station and hit a concrete wall at the end of the tunnel...that was Moorgate Station in the City of London in 1975, over 40 passengers died...

At birth you enter into a new stage in life, it is just another chapter, after having existed within our mother's womb. At death, your soul enters into another chapter of your existence, your soul is liberated into eternity. You are born when you leave your mother's body and your soul is born when it leaves your body. This is the continuity of life.

What do you have when you are within your mother's womb?, money, mobile phones, gold chains, shoes, computers or cars?, none of those, you are fed by your mother, food, drink, love, kindness, even music and nice words. Your soul deserves a similar treatment, before it abandons your body, when your body dies. Do you feed your soul with kindness, love, good words, truth, kindness...? Is this what you do Simon?
Watch out!, this is not a religious text, nor intended to teach or give examples, surely many more people have experiences, that in essence would be similar. These are real stories, names and places have been changed.

FIRST PART

1
The Origins In South America

Simon was a quiet boy, calm, without being brilliant in any respect, we could say "normal", with routines at school, studies, games, family, friends and mischief. A scorpion in training. Why should Simon have to go through the experiences that one never has to go through?, those events that one reads in books, see in movies, TV or the Internet?

Enjoys sea fishing, one day I left home early with my friend David, as the tide was suitable for a relaxing day of fishing. We were on the shore, at the foot of the mouth of a river, we had good fishing in that place at other times, but we this morning we had been there for three hours and nothing … so hungry and thirsty, I asked David if he would agree to leave the fishing trip for the day, to go and have some ice cream. I really prefer fruit, but I knew David would agree with ice cream and I really wanted was to go away from there.

We had only walked about 500 meters, when we heard a very loud noise, like the sound of a river carrying rocks, but louder … yes, it was the river that brought an avalanche with it and overflowed, we ran back to where we had been fished, the rocks where we had been trying to fish for three hours, were no longer there, they were gone ... do you understand Simon?

My brother Albert was my greatest friend, a good example, studious, intelligent, helpful, fair and very honest. Alberto had appearance of a Professor, he was six years older than me, corrected me when I was astray, but knew how to correct me, with good, kind words, he was like that every day, he protected me and I respected him. In a period of twelve months, life took us very far, the two of us ended up in Europe, studying in different Countries, he was in Germany and I was in England. New languages, new and different environments; other friends, customs, food and different climates.

That was good fellowship, sometimes he visited me in England, he only had to pay for his round trip, as the stay was on my account. When I travelled to Germany, I knew I just needed to pay my ticket and then the travel money was for him to finance, Alberto, not only studied but worked part-time in a motorcycle factory and earned good money.

2
Getting to Know Europe

Each trip in Europe produced a lot of knowledge, in my very first trip I decided I had to cover the maximum possible distance, perhaps because maybe "I would never have another chance to visit" (lol ... how wrong was I), with all the experiences that came later ... travel with extra-terrestrial beings and to get to "visit" the other "life" after death and then come back to tell about it ...do plants grow there? Do they sell mineral water and chocolates in these places...?

Amazing, but my experiences took me to places I had not intended to get to, nor had I imagined or dreamt and yes they were very different realities. As a student in Europe, traveling by train, I had searched and obtained a "pass", which was like a multiple ticket, allowing travel by virtually all trains in Europe, for a single price, very cheap indeed, travelled a lot and often sleeping on overnight trains, sometimes traveling from one place to another for four hours and I was back on the next train, technique I learned for sleeping and not having to pay for a hotel, or having to spend the night on the streets.

Getting to know and learn languages, people, customs, ways of living, a great eagerness to assimilate and sift whatever did not interest me, or what I knew was not good, that for sure, exactly, to differentiate between what I considered right and wrong, I became interested and absorbed what I wanted to keep and knew that I had simply to "accept" other views habits or ways, as I had no possibility to change others, I learned to appreciate life. I understood what was obvious, like those in the cold weather had to wrap up and those living in the heat, were people scantily dressed and cannot pretend to do the opposite, isn't it obvious, right...?

One night, my calculation failed, I arrived at Amsterdam's Central Station, in Holland, on a train that ended there, that was the last stop in the middle of the night and there was no other train leaving that Station until the morning, I walked around the city, until I was so tired and cold, that went into a public phone booth and I was starting there until I fell asleep. Bang, bang bang!... I felt on the glass of the phone booth, it was a policeman who told me I should not sleep in public phone booth, asked me to keep on walking...

After several days of travel, I returned to Munich, Germany, to Alberto's apartment, to shower, relax, narrate my adventures, to get some more money to keep traveling. Alberto had a very clean, comfortable, modern apartment, on a tenth floor, with a beautiful view of the city, parks and gardens, but with a small single bedroom, I slept on a mattress that we placed on the floor in the main room, the apartment was easy to clean, he was very tidy and cooked extremely well! (I mean that he cooked the meals that I liked ... ah, incidentally, that was where I learned to cook).

In April, Easter time, as the spring had started, I decided to go to Scandinavia, Sweden and Finland, there was a ferry crossing from Stockholm to Turku (Finland), I heard that Finnish girls went crazy when they saw a boy with black hair... I was curious to check it out ... it was true ... !!!, I fell asleep in the main hall in the ferry, together with the poor tourists, students, I was naive, very naïve..., I felt a little cold, but I went on the trip, just wearing a T-shirt and no change of clothes nor any jacket or jumper, BANG!!! BOOM!!!, BANG!!! I felt a noise that sounded as if the boat was breaking, however most passengers were just having fun on board (it was like a circus, people coming in and out of different rooms and halls), no one paid attention to the noises, BANG!!!, BOOM!!!, it continued, I looked for the way to the deck, I was scared, I thought something was happening, had the ship crashed and no one had noticed?, what was that loud continuous noise?, it was night, and from the deck, I saw and felt the thick ice on the sea, as the boat had become an "ice breaker", what horror!!!, the boat made its way on the ice, breaking it and I thought, and now ...what do I do next?

I had no coat, no money to buy anything, I had just enough money to buy my food for the duration of my trip, I could not go back ... I had no choice but to go inside the boat, the ferry seemed like a luxury liner and I continued travel, it was endless, we travelled all night, it very comfortable, but once in Finland, decided that to return by boat would not be the best choice for me, the shock had been too much, I took the train route back, that meant passing through the Arctic circle, so I kept almost all the time on the trains (more sheltered), just a few meters by foot, a short walk to cross the border between Finland and Sweden.

I met lots of people on the road, in villages, in cities and sometimes got invited to spend a night in the house of the very friendly and welcoming locals, sleeping in a bed gave a sensational recharge "batteries" feeling..! The heat from the radiators, fireplaces, they were so welcoming and warm places, home-cooked meals ... mmmm ... yummy!!! and the people so friendly, I wanted to stay there ...! My very first sleigh ride, it seemed as if it was winter but it was spring already, I was showing my "warmth" in my summer clothes (hot Latino blood... lol...). In southern Sweden, I saw the sandy beaches and "dreamed" to enjoy those beaches one summer, the beaches and the sea are my passion.

3
The Trip To Greece

On the return journey from Sweden to Denmark, the complete train rolled into the Ferry to cross the sea, novelty, very clever!!!, I should see the deck, would it have snow?, Would there be ice on the sea?, Would it be another icebreaker? I left the train compartment and climbed the stairs to the deck. Where are you travelling? Asked Erika, to Munich I said, I return to the apartment, where my brother Alberto lives, ok, let's travel together, she suggested to me, I'm going to Athens, what? Athens in Greece?, that's very far!!!, yes, the journey there takes three days, but it's very pretty, I was there once and I want to know more about Athens, Erika told me.

She spoke a lot about Greece and what a wonderful time she had had there, she was very excited with the idea of visiting Greece again, she convinced me to go with her all the way. In Munich the train had a major stop-over and it was staying at the station for two hours and I took advantage of this, ran to see my brother Alberto in his apartment and told him I had met Erika, a Swedish girl and wanted to travel with her to Athens, what???!!!..., are you mad???!!!, you're really crazy!!!, well, here's some money, I'll go with you to the station, I want to meet that Erika ... timing was just right and continued the tour with my new Swedish friend, we talked a lot, shared the little food we had, including water, all with the idea to save money, we did not want to run out of cash during the trip.

The train compartment had 6 seats, three facing forward and three backwards, at night, the seats stretched down and became horizontal beds. During one of the nights, the lights in the compartment were switched on and a uniformed person, like a soldier came in and said that he wanted to see our passports that was at the border with Yugoslavia. Where is your visa? He asked me in a badly spoken English, half asleep I said, I do not have one, you need a visa to travel to Yugoslavia, the official informed me and you can buy it right here, the inspector demanded some money and he continued inspecting other passports. Luckily I had the money that Alberto had given me, I paid for the visa, gave me back my passport and then we continued travelling.

We were very tired and after three days and three nights, the train arrived in Athens, after midnight, with sweltering heat, there were about 40 degrees Centigrade, the heat and the high humidity at the station, were really not so welcoming to us that had travelled such a long distance and were not used to it. On the platform at the Station, there were people who recommended a "Youth Hostel", hat sounded good, cheap and somewhere we could both get some sleep. Erika had room number 6, and I got room 11. I entered the room, it was dark and the room had about 5 bunk beds (those with two levels), the first bed, right in front of the door, had the upper bed unoccupied, the heat seem to be getting stronger!, we felt so tired!, as I walked into the room, I noticed the person sleeping on the bottom bed was completely naked on top of the mattress, face down, the heat was unbearable. I decide to occupy the top part of the first bunk bed, just a mattress, no sheets, it didn't matter, everyone seem to be lying just on the mattress. I took off my clothes and got on the top bed. After a few minutes I felt someone coughing in the room and I thought that was a woman coughing ... the two people came into the room, women, and they went to other beds, I thought, I was given room number eleven, is it that I got into the wrong room?, I looked at the person on the bottom bunk and that was another woman, she had turned around and was now facing up ... I looked around, I looked at every bed and I concluded that the room was mixed. As soon as it became light, I jumped out of bed, took my clothes went into the shower, went for breakfast and walked all day with Erika.

I only spent three days in Athens and then began the return journey by train to Munich, I said goodbye to Erika and we wished each other good luck, we'd had a great time together while travelling, we had fun and we had seen many new places, lot, I was again out of money... needed food and rest ... I took the train back to Munich from Athens, when we entered Yugoslavia, a guard came into the compartment and asked to view the passports and he asked me where was my visa to visit Yugoslavia?, there it is !!!, I showed him my passport, opened on the page where my visa had been stamped and he told me, that visa was used, as it only allowed one entry into the Country .... Young man, you need to buy a visa for each entry into the country ... the world stopped on me, I was quite literally without any money... he told me that if I did not pay the visa, I would have to get off the train and had to go to jail...!!!, I was speechless, "frozen", I felt I was falling to a bottomless pit, I had no money and there was no other solution, would I have to go to jail?, in the train compartment there were only very old people, only two elderly couples who did not speak any English at all and there was also a young girl who was blonde, tall and "perfect" measurements, she was German, Rita, who told me in English: take, here's the money for your visa ... like a saviour angel, are you sure? I asked, yes, unless you want to go to jail? She inquired. I took the money and paid the visa, we continued the whole trip talking about all the good things about Germany, its people and what places I really needed to visit, she said I had to go to Berlin, but not on that trip, she lived in a village, a hour before arriving in Munich, come, stay and rest at home tonight and you can continue your trip to Munich tomorrow, it's late.

Ok, left the train at her village, a quiet area, well-kept gardens, people greeted us on the street and she took me to her home, it was an apartment on the second floor, where she lived alone, her house was small, but very cosy, had only a single room, which was living, dining and study, there was just one bedroom, the heating was very relaxing. She prepared a hot tub and I had a very relaxing bath ... ahh what a difference that made!!, Rita prepared some food, it was meat with cheese and tomato sauce, we drank a bottle of wine (or was it two? ...) she said that she had saved it for a "special occasion". Later in the evening, she offered me her bed, so that I could have a good rest... and when I woke up the next day, with her beside me ...ahh ...learning Simon?, yes, I learned... there are people who help you along the way, but do not necessarily want money back...

4
Early Moral Ideas

Early in life I had contact with a Catholic religious group in South America, good things were heard about them, but also some extreme views, oops!!!, I did not like, nor do I like anything extreme!!!, Good ideas, clear, which served me much in complementing my background of moral principles and good and wellbeing of others, nothing wrong, it has served me well, to keep me on the right track, through detours and shortcuts, but generally on the right track.

I think they have been and are, many of the fundamental ideas that I learned in that time, that have kept me away from being idle, close to prayer. Actually attended Mass daily for a long time and that didn't make me ill. I attended many talks of religious formation, say of moral principles that later helped me a lot, met a lot of interesting people, including three guys whom later went to Rome and became priests there.

In Europe, I kept on meeting people from that group, thankfully!!!, As in my day to day I met each case... each one was really a case.... the people of the religious group "focused" me on my path and helped me to have clear ideas and ideals, as there was alcohol, drugs, sex and other "attractive" ways, but not necessarily "good". Ahhh of course, there was fun, punks were born (coloured hair, Mohawk hairstyles!!!... "Streaking" became fashionable, "skinheads", well, I must admit it, even I had such long hair, most people would not recognize me...

During a holiday period as a student, I had to find alternative accommodation, I had heard of a Scandinavian run youth hostel for girls, which sometimes took on boys and occasionally other nationalities. Ahhh ... that's what I call good luck!!!, They accepted me, the place was small but had about 30 girls and only 8 men staying there. As good traditional place, they closed and locked the door at 11pm. The theatre has always been one of my passions and in London the theatre is a great attraction, with quality acting and marvellous presentation. So, one Friday night I organized to attend the theatre with Susan and Erika, two cute girls, Susan was blond and blue eyes, while Erika was red hair and green eyes, they lived in the same place where I was staying. The play at the theatre was a musical and like most plays in London, really impressed us. After the theatre, we decided to go to a Chinese restaurant, since the theatre was in the middle of "China Town" and there were plenty of good oriental restaurants. After dinner, Susan asked to be excused, because she was going to see her boyfriend that night. Along with Erika, we headed back to our hostel, but when we arrived, all the lights were off, it was almost midnight and although we rang the bell, the door, not even the windows were opened ... Of course, in winter we were not going to sleep on the street, so we went to a hotel that was close by and we requested a room with two beds, because as students, we could not afford two rooms. The head of the reception told us that he only had one room, but with a double bed ... well, we take it, then we agreed on the "rules of the game" Simon ... do you understand...?

5
Carolina Came Into My Life

I read several books on cultivation of your inner soul and found in them very valuable thoughts. I learned to do small things, close to yourself and without any major ambitions to change the world... I learned to pray for others, especially for someone who was at that time near to me, well, just at that time it was my classmate at school Carolina. We shared the same desk in the classroom at school and we respected each other, we had very different personalities, young people full of illusions, both could be said were of "good heart", we discussed some ideas of books and religious issues, deep discussions and we keep arguing until today...!

I decided to assume a challenge, to do something good for her and to always pray for her, without anyone knowing, I continued praying for her happiness and maintained doing so, one, five, ten, twenty years, even without seeing her during all that time, really without any personal interest, even when each of us was married to another person and even after that, when we were both "unmarried", after all that time "click", we saw each other again, we both felt "love at first sight" it was mutual and instantly. Without realizing I had prayed for her happiness and that happiness ended up being with me. Do you understand Simon?

Each event has such a close link to the rest of your life, the explanation is equally as complex...

During a re-union gathering for former students, after 25 years of having graduated from school, I saw Caroline again, we never separated ever since. During our romance, there were "weekend meetings", with international travel, I remembered what my brother Alberto had said: "what???!!!..., are you mad???!!!, you're really crazy!!!".

Everything happened without any "premeditation". Events were very fast, someone made a comment during the re-union gathering, if there is anyone that has something to say, they'd better say it now or keep quiet forever...

Caroline had two sons and a failed marriage, I had no children, but did have a failed marriage.

I remember one day, whilst fishing in the coast of Mexico, I had some very clear thoughts, that I had been married "forever", thus I could not be "seeking" for another person, on the other hand, I could not imagine to see myself on my own for the rest of my life. That was the essence of it all, how could I live together with the idea of continuing with an acquired compromise, no longer feasible? to continue eternally with the idea of being "alone" in life?, surely over time, people's customs change, people's interests have different priorities, fashion changes, what was previously long hair, is now short hair and the "home" for ever is now the home of "now", things are no longer perceived to be for all of your life...is it the same for people's relationships?...in reality, nothing has changed, only people's perceptions have changed, we continue being the same beings from the time we are born until we die, we are begotten and later we continue the path with our souls, we forge our own future and destiny, full of mistakes and successes...do you remember Simon...?, do you understand Simon...?

Ahhh...I remember, I did not even want to listen to that Spanish priest, I didn't like him at all, I thought his manners were not respectful, even "dis-respectful", dry, almost arrogant and gave me the impression that he did not listen, that he only wanted to indoctrinate in his own way. It has to be said that his ideas were simple, very clear, perhaps did not show in his face, nor in his attitude...yes, his body was one and his soul was a different thing. His body, his gestures, expressions, caused me rejection, whilst his soul gave attraction, peace and simplicity (hummm...qualities that later I understood...).

After a while, I began having some confidence in this "priest-person" from Spain, well I actually learned from him, how to treat God with great confidence, in the same manner that I treat my friends, my best friend, my partner, in whom I trust and not question, not as a far away, remote being.

God, why don't you listen to me?, why don't you grant me what I believe to be "just"?, being right in earthly affairs, to be good or to do good things, isn't necessarily give you the earthly success, I understood!!!

The reward comes later...If your wife becomes pregnant and was a case of oops...!!! (Not scheduled at that time...), you get your reward later, perhaps at the time you do not realize or understand, but you can be sure that in time it will arrive...

I have had several bad experiences that have made me very disappointed for various reasons, about beliefs that we all assume to be true and real. Disillusion surely has been for most to discover that Father Christmas was not whom we thought he was...do you understand Simon? My disillusions grew with time, over the earthly "justice", legal actions, including a very big dispute in Great Britain, against an Insurance Company, having had to ask for help from the Ombudsman...only to discover how "dirty" and biased the system was, the protection for the companies or the more "powerful", anyway, I have experiences of several other cases of this nature. Telling the truth, abide by the rules, does not necessarily "open the doors" in this world, however, the Devine Justice is a different matter!!!...that always exists and is always right...!!!, the important issue is to obtain the "ticket" for the soul to reach "heaven" and not "hell", I assure this through my own experience, what???, yes, through my own experience...!!!

6
The Landslide – Survive

When I was a teenager, some schools organized day trips, in groups of 10, 20 or even 30 students, together with one or two teachers, getting to the countryside or the beach, sightseeing or visiting historic places. We were a group of about 20 teenagers and arrived by bus to a very nice spot, near a river, at the foot of the mountains in a narrow valley. The river was flowing fast and it was noisy, very cold water, the place was really attractive. The day was with blue skies, plenty of sunshine, it was glorious!!! There had not been any rain for a while, everything was dry and there was little vegetation. All young, dynamic people, full of energy and adventurous, we decided on a small group of three to do some exercise, climbing part of the mountain, the land was aid, bare, pebbles and rocks, as we climbed, the views were getting better, across and down the valley, our friends appeared smaller and smaller as we climbed higher up the mountain.

Suddenly, there was a loud noise that seemed like an explosion, we paused, we looked down to the river, across the mountain, up and down the valley and then up the mountain, oops!!!, OOPS!!! Something cad collapsed and there was an avalanche coming towards us!!!, descending very fast towards us, pebbles, rocks bouncing all over the place and in our direction. We were horrified and looked quickly at our choices, to go back down was not a choice, we had climbed up too much and had no time to return, in fact there was no time to go to the right or the left, the avalanche was approaching fast...we were trapped in the path of the falling rocks!!!, what could we do?, about five meters from where we were, the was a huge rock, about a meter and a half in diameter, we shouted, "there!!, run!!!" and we lied down behind the rock, looking for protection, as if that rock could "protect" us from being hit by the falling ones...!!!

One laid on the ground, the second was above and I was on top, watching and describing the trajectory of the "projectiles", we prayed so that our lives may be "saved"...we thought it would be very difficult not to be hit by one of those rocks. The situation was getting worse, the avalanche was about to hit the area where we were, there were some huge rocks flying past and bouncing all over and around us. I saw an enormous rock, about the same size of the one that was "protecting" us bouncing rapidly in the direction of my eyes and I saw it bounce, looked at the trajectory and I announced to my friends, this rock will hit us!!, prepare yourselves, this looks like "the end"!!!, I saw the rock passing just about thirty centimetres above my head, just in time, as did all the other rocks and stones, they all avoided us, we were spared!

We were so scared that we could not talk, not say a word until the next day, the terror had been enormous... The Big Boss was giving us signals, however, not in English, Spanish, nor in Japanese, it was in "his manner", however, what did he want to tell us? What did he want to prove to us? At that time, due to immaturity, I only thought about the "now" and not beyond. We were saved!, were we saved?!...you saved your body...and did you worry about your soul?...do you understand Simon?

7
Karen In Scotland

Quiet, introverted, not speaking the language, not knowing anyone in (the cold weather (well, shall I say really freezing), with rain (should I say with continuous heavy rain), living in a small village, far from the cities, almost penniless, in short, hardly able to interact with people, to make or keep friends, but even then, there was a chance to feel physical and emotional attraction, Karen was a very slim local girl, red-head long, smooth hair, Scottish, with a very special smile, patient and understanding, I learned thanks to her, customs of her Country, meals, drinks (Whisky), dances, ahh... her dancing was very sensual..., she also taught me a lot of the English language and its differences with the "Scottish" variety.

Karen was my first girlfriend in Great Britain. A lovely friendship, youthful and clean. Then when I continued with my studies, I moved south, into England, we were separated due to the distance, our friendship literally became more "distant", our encounters were less frequent, but very significant, appreciation grew, we talked a lot, we shared.

My journey through life took me to another city, Manchester, in Great Britain, an industrial city that was being transformed, modernized, certain industries being essential for the changeover from coal energy, originating in the underground coal mines to natural gas sourced at the bottom of the North Sea. That was going to be the start of a new energy, cheaper and cleaner than coal.

New friendships, new experiences, new vision of life, a sense of growth in my background...always an introvert, calm, sensible, cautious character.

The day of the move arrived...with the packed suitcases, the books, organize the clothes and all my bits and pieces in the new room that I had in the students hostel, which was mainly a female student hostel, where only some 30% of the lodgers were guys. The building was modern, clean, with well-kept gardens, kitchens, bathrooms, common leisure areas, very comfortable, although here were male and female wings in the building, the bedrooms were small but overall everything was quite adequate to study in a warm and well lit area. Uff...!!! How very tired I am...enough for the first day and I think it would be a good idea to go out for a walk at least around the block...ohhh...!!! The block was huge!, I walked for a long time, the evening was light and pleasant, very few people on the street, nice gardens, big houses, I was curious about my new neighbourhood, I was walking and enjoying every moment, after some twenty minutes walk, I saw two girls walking in the opposite direction and as we came closer, the crossed over the road, to be on my side of the street and I imagined they would ask me for directions somewhere...and just my luck, I had just arrived in the area...so, they stopped me and on...ohh nooo...they didn't want to ask me for directions, one of the girls announced that her best friend had her birthday that day!! And asked would I compliment her on her birthday? What...??? Did I hear...I didn't even know her, I thought...I said Happy Birthday, but before I could finish saying that, she was collecting her birthday present, which was a real deep kiss... kkk???xxx?? I was shocked, but I learned in more detail, something new about the English "tongue"...hahaha...!!!That was not in my book of "experiences", shall we say that event made me realize that my book of experience was a lot wider than I had previously thought or imagined...do you understand Simon?

The hostel had certain "rules", schedules of times to arrive home, times to prepare meals, but of course there was always the excitement of some boy spending the night in the bedroom of a girl or vice versa and thinking that "no one would ever know." !!! ... lol ... the walls were very thin and the bathrooms and showers were common, separated cubicles for girls and boys, but sometimes the legs seen "did not correspond" ...hahaha ... "no one would ever know"... !!!

"Good morning", you arrived early today...!!! that was the comment to indicate...and you thought we didn't know where you spent the night...?

My lectures always started punctually on time, I found that the courses and teaching methods were very well organised, we used to have small study groups, just three to five students. We enjoyed comfortable, ample classrooms very well equipped, friendly and very professional lecturers, it was really a very pleasant atmosphere.

During the holidays, like most students, had to get a temporary job, anything was good, the higher the pay, the better...thus, I managed to get a job, as a salesman in a men's clothing store. Hey...!!! That's where I learned to say, not the whole truth, because when a client tried two or more pieces of clothing, always the piece that had a red sticker "fitted better" and that was simply because those with the red stickers gave me a higher commission...hahaha...also the clothes with the yellow spot were always the "second best"...you guessed, those gave me the second best commission...!!! That was a difficult experience, trying to avoid telling lies... do you understand Simon?

During my next holidays, I was lucky to get another job, better paid, that was in a private Security firm. My first assignment, the first day, was to be in the back of a security armoured van, I had to hand over the bags with money and documents to my colleagues, through a small window. The armed guys working in the front of the van had to take the bags to the banks we were visiting on or scheduled route...I only lasted one day in that position, because I passed the wrong bag to the guys and they were not happy to be walking in and out of the bank, carrying the cash. The following day I reported by phone to the firm's HQ and they asked me to do night shift as a guard in the Houses of Parliament in London, that was easy and I was doing that for two weeks. The following week they asked me to go to the Foreign Office that was exciting, very close to Parliament, there were a lot more people coming in and out of that building and I received good money then. At the start of my next week, I reported again by phone to my HQ, with my employee number 8789612. The Security firm would then give me my next assignment. The guy at the other end of the line confirmed ahh...you were in the Houses of Parliament and then the Foreign Office, very well, I think I am going to send you to the Foreign Office again this week, what is your name?, he asked me....so, I gave him my name...oops...!, you are not British?, no...oops... They don't like any foreign nationals to work in those places, I very quickly added, well, don't tell them and I won't tell them either...and nobody will know the difference...!!!, my accent was so good that he just laughed and told me, ok go back to the same place...!! Do you understand Simon?!

8
Claire In Manchester – Gas, National Priority

Learning to wash clothes, iron them, to cook and to make money, this was because I obtained a scholarship to finance my studies, ahh...I even had to take care of the soap, the money for bus fares...clothing...mmm...well, for everything, had to administer time for study, homework, entertainment, games, had to include everything, as the scholarship had to cover all my expenses, well, I had the extra money from the holiday jobs and a full time one I managed to obtain, related to my studies. I was on a practical experience job in a firm, manufacturing equipment for the North Sea Oil platforms, this industry became of National Priority in Great Britain, at the start of the 1970's, when the price of Crude oil rocketed up, at the time of the oil crisis and the strengthening of the Opec (Organization of Petroleum Exporting Countries).

There were National Strikes, stoppages, protests, but the Industry that continued strong was that of the North Sea Oil, I managed to put together some money and went to Latin America on a tour with an English girlfriend, Claire, shall we say the typical "gringa", Claire, with whom we got on extremely well, but what had happened is that I had absorbed in two years a lot more of the European habits that I would have imagined or would have realized. I travelled with my girlfriend, together, but without noticing that for everyone else around, this was "strange", that a couple would travel together, without being "officially" being declared as a "couple", without having married.....bah...!! How silly, I thought,...depending on the atmosphere and the surroundings, what we should always consider is the surroundings and not just to keep oneself on the stage, one should neglect the points of view of the others, what one has "sieved" in life and is useful to oneself, not necessarily is useful to others, nor are they going to see it in the same manner as oneself....remember Simon....a modern art painter, is not the same as a pain restorer...nor a dentist is the same as a psychologist...we are not all alike, we have different tastes, objectives, different talents and each of us will try to do the best we can, even better, without interfering with the others, of course, showing them why we are in one way or in another...our interests, our points of view are, without any doubt, all different, they are all correct, each in their own individual path, all with the same aim, do you understand Simon?...in the cold weather, you need to wrap up and in the heat, the opposite...!! Police!!!, what does the police want with us in this remote village?, it is night-time and we are very tired, we want to go to sleep...passports?, why...? We have not done anything wrong...ahh, to be in the same room and not be married?, this "breaks" their rules??...hey!!, the world really has different rules for each region...well, one travels and one learns, every minute is an experience and a page on one's "book of life".

The story is the same, after such closeness and living together, time also separated me from Claire, life has separated me from my loved ones, for different reasons...after the separation, the physical distance, not of the ideas, feeling, lessons of life, everything is cumulative, all that is "filtered" and is in "good soil", sooner or later will give fruit, even if one cannot be there to "harvest" the results, that is the beauty, that is so rewarding, to know that you did something good and not to be sorry about not having done it.

Time and destiny took me to London to continue with my studies, once again everything was new, dearer, more impersonal, bigger city and with new challenges, a lot more to know and to learn. Through time, experiences marked the path, the way, the guidance was unique but the destiny was not clear, the meaning of life was one to "let the time flow" and not "set the time".

I saw Karen ever less frequently, very seldom, the friendship continued, our friendship was profound and sincere, travelling from Scotland to London was a very long journey, expensive and tiresome, we enjoyed it whenever it was possible.

9
The Sudden Death

One of the things I always prayed to God, was for him to protect me from a sudden death, that is because I did not want to lose the opportunity to go to Heaven, that nice place that I had so much heard about...surely it would be a "cool" place (awesome!! As some people say...!!!), surely too good to be missed by something silly, rather than falling into that horrible place called "hell"...that place where they say that even smells of sulphur...and is very unpleasant...hey!!, No..!!!, no way!!!, I was afraid!!!. I once heard the story of a soccer player in Europe, he is said to have always prayed in a similar manner to my own prayers, to avoid sudden death and to have the opportunity to ask for forgiveness and in that way to be "saved", but he died very suddenly in an air crash, one of the most sudden forms of dying...!!! How?, so God did not listen to him?, or he didn't hear the poor guy asking not to be taken away suddenly without a chance to ask to be pardoned...? Or was it the contrary, God heard him and took him away when he was ready, without any suffering, because he was always "ready"?

My case was very similar, I was taken in a very sudden "instant" manner, but the "scare" was double, because

I was taken to experience both places, the very pleasant and the horrible one...!!!, I returned to finish my journey and to make sure that the next time I had to be ready with my "ticket" to eternal life, but for the "good" side (heaven) and not the "bad" side (hell). How was this done?, is it easily done?, can anyone do it?

In the Novel "the Moon is on the Moon", there was a story about a journey to the moon, discovering entrances through the craters into the nucleus, inside it was like a mini-planet, with buildings, vehicles, cities and looking up (looking out), the sky could be seen freely, in other words, the moon's surface was transparent when look at from inside the moon. That was a totally fictitious, interesting, but "invented" or "made up", the experiences told in this book have not been made up, "unfortunately" they are all true and real events!!

I think that my experience was what is death and to discover that dying is no more than another form of "sleep", one stops to see through the eyes, stops thinking consciously, one stops listening, but one remains existing, one breaths, one has "life", life does not stop there, it is a different form of life, life doesn't end there, life of a different kind continues, just as the life one has inside one's mother's womb is also of a different kind, we have a life (or existence) that continues precisely in a continuous form, without interruption, even before we are born, during our life in our bodies and then continues, after the death of our bodies, in a continuous form, as the life of our soul into eternity.

We learned to believe that the inert beings, like stones or the plaanets are non-intelligent beings, not developed, when in reality those are the beings that are "perfect", they no longer need to develop any more, like we do, we humans are imperfect beings. Planets move around the universe fulfilling their mission to participate in the symphony of the cosmos, where every part of it follows their perfect laws, the perfect attraction between planets, some maintain their proximity and others are pushed apart. Rocks, the stones have their properties that typify their qualities that are their characteristics, they do not behave in different forms, like we humans do, so for example, smoky quartz (eliminates fear, depression and promotes positive, pragmatic thinking), amethyst (increases the production of hormones, helps in purifying blood), Jasper (promotes connection to the spiritual world), agate (has great power to solve problems and gives support in difficult times), each of the stones, even water and minerals, they all have their properties and they fulfil their functions completely, with their invariable characteristics.

Some of us humans are good in sports, others in mathematics, others in caring of the sick and we all complement each other. We humans have not yet reached the level of development that the stones and other beings have already attained, they have already conquered the full magnitude of their functions.

As a child I sometimes "submerged" in "travel" into the world's smallest forms, for me, an ant was little, one could see as if through a microscope and dive into the world of littleness and then look the other way, see others, the humans as giants and then the elephants, as super extra mega beings, but we all live in the same space. The ants in their world, which is very limited, cannot travel between continents and back, but the birds can and do with much greater skill and ease than we humans and without us really knowing how to explain nor understand them.

10
The Ticket To... Eternity

On Friday 28th February 1975, I was going to have lectures at the City of London Polytechnic, I got up that morning some two hours earlier than usual. My first lecture was at ten thirty in the morning, but I decided I would go into the City, earlier than usual and then go to the library, to study, that was unusual for me, but that morning I had the best intention to go there to study before my lectures. I was living alone in a bed-sitter, a mini-apartment with just one room that was living, dining and bedroom. There was a tiny space for the kitchen. I lived on the second floor of a big house that had been converted into small flats and bedsitters, as it was very common in London. There were five of those flats in the house.

I walked to Turnpike Lane underground station in Hornsey, I went on the Piccadilly Line train travelling south and eventually at Finsbury Park station, I changed onto the Northern Line train, which departed at 08:39 am from the first station, that train whose destiny would change the rest of my life and that of many other people and families.

The tube train had departed from Drayton Park in North London, for the short ride which had as a final stop, on a direct route, Moorgate, which was also the last stop on that particular tunnel, underneath the financial centre of the City of London.

I knew that when arriving at Moorgate, the escalator to exit the station was near the front of the train, in fact, right by the middle doors of the first coach and for this reason, I decided to board the train through the middle set of doors of the front coach and I found an empty seat just by the middle set of doors, with a glass panel to my left side. I was sitting facing the side of the train and the train was moving towards my left. As usual, there was silence within the compartment, no one was talking, the only sound was that of the running train on the metal rails and that of the doors when they opened and closed. A very typical scene on the London underground, sometimes someone talking in a low voice, each of us in their "own little world". I ws reading a newspaper and did not realize how far we were from Moorgate station, there was nothing out of the common, nothing strange, everything was quiet, until suddenly the train shuddered and that short and sharp movement, made my body lean forward and lower the newspaper in such a way that I saw a woman sitting opposite me, I only saw her face and it was at that instant that the lights went off. I have the image of the face of this woman very clear in my memory, even today, I still remember her face, at that moment her expression was peaceful, slight smile, she was attractive, innocent looking. She did not survive the event.

Everything turned pitch black, there was a tremendous crashing sound at the moment of the impact, it was an almighty sound, like an explosion, twisting metal and glass breaking, no one shouted, nor cried, everything happened in a fraction of a second, the time it takes you to inhale air into your lungs when breathing, for me and I am sure for many others, it was all over in less than an instant.

Following the sudden impact, I lost the notion of time, of location, of life itself, of everything...I felt that I "ascended" into the space, I was being "absorbed", floating upwards into a space where it was all white, peaceful, it was not shiny white like the sun reflecting on the snow, nor like the white of clean bed sheets, it was a different whiteness, I was floating in the air, I was suspended in a vacuum, I was very happy, looking at the relaxing whiteness around me. I felt attracted, like through magnetism, I was being "pulled" gently up, "absorbed" slowly and I was letting myself go up, ever deeper into the whiteness, I wanted to continue, I looked around me and everything was marvellous, calm, attractive, inviting, there was no sound, that place irradiated peace, all was full of positive sensations. There were no sharp brilliance, nor were walls, oceans, trees or buildings, there were no people either. Everything was of a uniform colour, very relaxing, clean and pure. I did not see anyone, but I knew I was not alone, there was no solitude, I felt I was in good company. Just as a child is attracted by a sweet, that "whiteness" attracted me and I continued to let myself go, I was getting closer and closer, I did not know where I was, nor why I was there or where I was going, the magnificent whiteness continued to attract me and I was pleased with it "absorbing" me, it was never ending…, it was an eternal pleasure. It was just like when you close your eyes and everything is uniform, when you are in total darkness and you see everything uniform, only that everything there was white and full of positive sensations.

After a while, I cannot say how long, again in an instant I felt that I was descending, falling into an unending depth, until I turned up in another place, very hot, full of loud screams, it was like being tortured, it was horrible and unpleasant, that place was extremely scary and in total darkness, I did not want to be there, the place was absorbing me down, I wanted to repel that fall, I wanted to get away from that attraction, it was a torture for me and I could no nothing to stop being "swallowed" down. It was like when a child sees a lion and he gets scared and does not want to get any closer, but wants to "run away" in the opposite direction. I was terrified, I do not remember any smells, not even that smell of "sulphur"…that does not mean that there was no smell, just that I do not remember any.

I had been unconscious, "dead?", I do not have any other additional "terrestrial" memories, from the moment of the impact of the train against the end of the tunnel and having seen the face of the woman sitting opposite me, woman that I might have met sometime, it might have been an "angel" that with his presence, might have wanted to give me a message, she died in the accident.

After the two experiences, of both of those journeys that I remember very clearly, the two places that I was taken to "see", which I am convinced were heaven and hell, eventually, the very next thing I remember was a shout from someone "is there anybody else there?" and there was total silence, my "conservation instinct" (just to call it something), made me shout back "YES, I am here!!!", but I did not know why I was shouting, nor where I was or what had happened. The distant voice shouted again "can you move?", I realized I had my hands next to my shoulders and on the floor, so I tried to lift myself up but I could not, it appears that I was face down and on the floor. I was not totally conscious, I did not know where I was, so I shouted back "NO, I cannot move!!!", I had a lot of pain in my chest and that didn't allow me to move. I did not remember anything, nor the accident, or anything of my life, nothing. Then I heard the distance voice again, shouting an instruction to me "cover your face up!!! And we'll get you out!!!" I still had no notion of time or anything around me, everything was totally dark. Very obediently, I crossed my hands behind my head, I could not feel anything I could not hear anything of what was going on around me, everything was still totally dark I was practically unconscious like being asleep.

The next thing I remember is that someone was injecting me something into my hand and then that person was raising my body, he was holding me from under my arm pits and asked me to secure my hands behind his neck, I asked him "what is your name?", he said "my name is David", I asked him "David, who are you?" and he replied "I work for the Rescue Services", I continued saying "thank you David", but really, even today, I do not know why I was saying these things, because I did not know where I was, nor what had happened. Was it all just a dream? Who was really this "David"? where were we?, what had happened?…all these doubts, questions and gaps took years in getting answered and even then, only partially.

David handed me over to someone else and indicated me that I should now hold myself from the back of his colleagues' neck and I heard him say "mind his back and I think his leg is broken". The second guy, transferred me onto a third person and again my "conservation instinct" (to call it something) made me repeat "mind my back and I think my leg is broken", I really didn't feel anything, I was only semi-conscious, I didn't know yet where I was, nor what had happened, it was like a dream, but I just repeated what I had heard before. I was not in charge of the situation, I was simply being manipulated by others. I remember these events and the exact words even today.

On the Surface, at Street level, the first official message requesting help due to the accident, was to ask for one ambulance, because it appeared that the driver of the train might have been hurt. Three coaches of the train could be seen at Platform 9 of the station, with their lights switched off and the doors opened, there was black suit everywhere and it was getting difficult to breathe, at the end of the tunnel there was a fourth coach, at the entrance of the tunnel, but no one imagined that hidden behind was such a tragedy, that coach was slightly tilted up and had some broken windows. A medical student arrived, initially saw that some people had some minor injuries, but little by little he was forming the idea that there could be a large number of wounded and even some deaths and eventually the plan for major emergencies was put into operation, under the control of Scotland Yard, the coordinated work of three hospitals, ambulances, firefighters, doctors, nurses and an impressive host by Londoners, who behaved very supportive, sincere, generous and loving towards this accident.

The rescue services took 4 days to get to rescue the body of the driver, his driving cabin had been compressed into a space of only 15 centimetres, due to the force of the impact. In order to rescue some of the passengers towards the front of the train, steel bars had to be cut, they were from the train compartments, which were all twisted. Only manual saw blades could be used, because there was no more space for any bigger tools.

After several years of curiosity and patient investigation, I found out that the front coach of the train was reduced to about a third of it's total length and to half it's height, the second carriage, meanwhile had been embedded below the first car in that tiny space, by the sheer weight and speed, the third carriage of the train had little damage and the last three were not affected and passengers descended frightened, some beaten and not really knowing what had happened to the front of the train and into the tunnel.

That train had 6 coaches and a total of 96 meters in length and weighed 151 tons, carrying about 300 passengers (extra weight), in fact, due to the time of the day, the train was not at full occupancy, 43 passengers were killed and 74 were injured. This has been the railway accident on the London Underground with the highest number of fatalities, since its inception in 1863, the actual train had been built in 1938, it was only 8:46am when the accident occurred and that was not full "rush hour" for transportation to the city centre. It had been 7 minutes since it had started the journey from the start of the line.

The tunnel was 29 meters long, that was the length of the tunnel beyond the end of platform number 9 of the underground station at Moorgate, until the concrete wall, 1.5 meters thick, which was the end of the tunnel, that space contained two carriages and a half, each car was 16 meters long, so that 40 meters from the train were compressed into a space of 29 meters, the first car was compressed from the original 15 meters length into just 4.5 meters, a third of its length and half its height. The first carriage was bent in the middle, leaving the back raised and the second carriage embedded beneath the first coach. The third carriage rammed the rear of the second coach and in practical terms, it blocked access to the tunnel and the last three compartments were not greatly affected.

I have read that on the front carriage, 43 people died, a young girl (who was a policewoman) was rescued, but had to have amputated a foot before releasing her. I understand that there were no more survivors from the front carriage, other than us two, in fact, I do not understand. I am sure that the people who died on impact, didn't feel anything, because everything was very violent and fast, but I fear that other people, who did not die at the moment of impact, suffered a lot and lived a lot of pain, as the rescuers who were as super-human, must have suffered immensely.

The train driver should have slowed down to about 25 km per hour, before entering Moorgate Station, as it was the last station on the line, but it accelerated to about 60 km/hour at impact, the rail track had a downward slope towards the end of the tunnel, which made the train accelerate even more, as if it were an express train, leaving dazed a few passengers waiting for the train at Platform 9, they were waiting to take it on the journey back.

I read many years later that rescuers had a tough job to cut through metal, removing train pieces, even body parts, to move towards the front of the train. There were people trapped that were rescued as they advanced towards the front of the train. I read that rescuers had difficulty breathing because of the soot, the high temperatures, working without light or communication. The tunnel had only one entrance, which was where the train entered and the distance was very short to the concrete wall which represented the end of the tunnel, there was no other access. The event had stopped normal life in the City of London, which is normally busy, is the financial centre, where major banks, insurance companies are, the stock exchange, metal markets, grain markets and other important international organizations are based.

The station platform was 30 meters underground, the rescue service took a little longer to arrive because the first impression was that the train was short and his last three compartments were intact at the station, there seemed to be a little damaged the fourth compartment end of the platform, but it took some time before it was realized that, there were also two full carriages "hidden" inside the tunnel.

11
Is There Anybody Else There???

People of the rescue services worked in appalling conditions, some described it as being in a coal mine, there was soot everywhere, it was worse than a horror movie or the worst nightmare, rescuers had to pass through very small spaces, sometimes only 60 centimetres wide, both ways, to enter the tunnel and again to go out and remove the wounded, there was total darkness, I read that a doctor said that if there was a hell, that is how it would be. The dust and soot that had accumulated on the walls and ceiling for more than 100 years, constantly came off, no fresh air to breathe, rescuers wore masks, there were screams in the dark and then just silence, people had black faces, as if they were "African" or "Caribbean" but no, it was that everyone seemed to have received a black coating of that black powder.

Ventilation in the platforms 9 and 10 was with the movement of the trains, that drove the air from outside, when the trains stopped, air access stopped.

Inside the tunnel, in the dark, there were compressed bodies by the twisted metal, decapitated bodies, huge rats were attracted by so many mutilated bodies, blood and dirt, rescuers moved slowly, having no choice but stepping on bodies of dead people, knowing they could do nothing for them, someone commented that it was ethically wrong, but they knew that deeper into the depth of the tunnel, which had a single way in and out, were other people who could still survive and needed help, they had to get to them, the whole thing was unworthy, disgusting, but entirely worthy of those rescuers. It was reported that when a flashlight or tool was dropped to the floor, there was no way to recover them, they were absorbed by darkness, dust, debris, glass, metals and humans. The heat was unbearable, coffins with dead people were brought up to the surface through the escalators of the station, while other empty coffins were brought down through the escalators by the side, a horrendous scenario was described. That was not a TV film, nor cartoons or a fiction terror movie, it was all true facts, it was the pure and chilling truth, those were facts reported by people of the rescue services, medical staff and reporters and I transcribe their stories with tears in my eyes, my God spared me, protected me and prevented me to see or participate in the horrific and macabre scene, although I evoke them today, with much pain, crying, as if I was living those moments all over again.

Days after the accident I received a plastic bag in the hospital, with my blackened clothes, sooty clothing, shrunken after being so wet, sweaty and then reduced in size, it was "sui generis" as if it was not of this world, I received all my belongings complete, nothing was missing, except life as it was before.

There were blood stains, not mine, from other people, as if to remind me that I always had to care for them, remember them, help them or help their souls to get to enjoy eternity in peace and tranquillity. I had a great void in my life, I did not know what had happened, I remember bits, pieces of experiences that fail to complete the "whole", and to give continuity in my life. Does it mark you? Yes, totally. The void in my life lasted for many years, in the hospital I only read news from newspapers, there was no TV in the place where I was, I had to recompose those separate scenes and understand their meaning, little by little, with new signs and experiences, the "whole" started to take shape, although still incomplete and inexplicable.

The next scene I remember of the rescue is that a policeman was beside me, more than four hours had passed since the accident, while I was lying on a bed (or a stretcher) without even knowing where I was, the cop asked me my name, the name of a close relative or someone who could be informed of my situation, a phone number, so I gave him the name and number of friends in Scotland.

The Police phoned Scotland, my friends thought I had been arrested by the police for a crime, they had not heard the news, but the police informed my friends that I had been in a train accident and had been taken to Saint Bartholomew's hospital in London. My friends then called my brother Francisco in South America to give him the news. After work, he went to visit my mother at her home.

Very quickly the news was reported worldwide. My mother lived alone in South America and saw the news on TV, at home, an underground train had crashed in the centre of London. Immediately she thought that her son (me) had died there and began to cry. She told Francisco that she had seen a news flash and she was worried at the thought that I might be dead in such a horrific train accident that had happened in London, where there were many dead and wounded. My brother Francisco told her I had already phoned to say that I was not on the train and I was fine, of course my mother did not believe him, because that sounded weird, that I had phoned only to say that I had not been at that event. The next morning, Francisco went to my mother's house again, supposedly just "to have breakfast with her," which was already a much more rare event, and told my mother that I actually had a friend that had phoned to inform that I had indeed been in the train that had crashed, had suffered some injuries and was in hospital in London, being treated.

My mother cried inconsolably and said, "you lied to me yesterday and today you're probably lying to me again," she pleaded with him, "Tell me the truth now, Simon is dead ?, have you spoken to Simon ?", the answer was no, he had not spoken with me, there was no way he could do that. Francisco communicated with our other brother, Alberto, who lived in Munich, with whom I had such an affinity, I, being in the hospital, did not remember his phone number to communicate with him in Germany, and Francisco asked him urgently to travel to London to find out exactly what had happened, how I was and what I might need.

During the rescue, I was on a stretcher, trying to stay awake, as I was put very quickly in an ambulance that was waiting at the surface, in the street, someone told me to go to sleep, but I said "no, I do not want to sleep I've never been in an ambulance before, I want to see how it is ... !!!, I am very curious to experience what it's like being transported in an ambulance", but the truth is that I did not even hear the siren, I was unconscious again, still did not know where I was really or what was happening, I was in a state of shock, total ignorance of the facts. I read that due to the severity of the accident and the fact that there were so many victims, at hospitals in London and elsewhere many people formed queues to donate blood. There was an atmosphere of great solidarity, many, many people use the London Underground and this could have happened to anyone. It is generally said that these things always happen to someone else, never to yourself, well, that time, I happened to me.

I arrived at the Hospital, they had taken me to the of St. Bartholomew's, in the City of London, partially conscious and a doctor examined all my body, every part of it, all the fingers, fingernails, head, hair to remove broken glass, all the way to the feet, I could not lie down, I had a lot of pain in the chest and had banged my head, in the front, upper left corner of the forehead, in the corner of the front and could only sit up in bed, unable to lie down, they said I had a broken hip, a fracture of the sternum, head injuries, it was probably that blow to the head that made me "disappear from this world" and as a consequence went to "those intriguing places". Besides the severe pain in general throughout my body, due to the battering I received, a light cut on my head made me loose maybe just a single drop of blood. At the hospital, I was told I had to have an urgent operation to my left leg.

In all the confusion, I was told I had to sign a document, giving permission for an operation on his left leg. "Why?" I argued, "I am told that my hip is broken ... it's not my leg!" I protested in the middle of that semi-conscious state and still not knowing what had happened or where I was and why. Someone explained to me, that it was necessary to place a metal nail through my left leg, below the knee, to hang a weight from there, at the end of the bed and that weight would make the head of my leg bone avoid contact with hipbone, thus avoiding "damage" (scratches), the hip bone was broken in many "bits" similar to glass, but all the pieces were in their place, and we had to prevent the pieces from moving. Are you sure it's my left leg that needs the operation?", my "conservation instinct" really it seemed to be inspired by a "guardian angel", who looked after me, was leading me ask, because I noticed that there was a great deal of confusion around and I did not want to be a victim of an administrative error...

With only local anaesthesia and sitting on the bed (I could not to lie down because of the chest pain) and they could not send me to sleep, not knowing the exact extent of the blows to my head, I was holding, squeezing the hand of Gloria, a wonderful nurse (It seemed that crushed her hand ... hey!!!, pardon me!!!), I saw a large pointed steel "skewer", similar to those used as meat skewers in a barbeque...!!, I saw how the doctor inserted the "skewer" through my leg, below my left knee. And ouch.. !!!, when the metal point reached the bone, it felt like sticking a knife in a piece of wood, could feel my bone breaking under the pressure from the skewer! Ouch...!!!, it hurts!...

I woke up Saturday (the following morning), in the hospital's intensive care unit, with a nurse beside me, she showed me a newspaper and read my name on the first page. "Oh my God!!! What have I done?, have robbed a bank? Does my name appear on the first page of the newspaper...???" "Why?" I asked the nurse, she was puzzled, "were you not on the train?" she asked me, "train? What train?" I asked, as I pictured in my mind a surface Inter-city train.

She insisted asking me if I had been in the underground train that had crashed at Moorgate station. I do not remember anything!!! I recognized the name "Moorgate" that was the station I used to travel to often to attend my classes, but did not remember being there recently. Gradually I realized what had happened, while reading the newspaper and the nurse explained to me, was all unreal, it did not seem to be true, the "dream" seemed to continue.

In the hospital, I received phone calls from people whom I had never met before, asking about my condition. I received many flowers, fruits, "get well" cards, "good health and speedy recovery" from children, religious groups, the Salvation Army, members of the City of London police offered help, people I did not know and just found out that I was a foreigner, injured on that train, it was all new to me and a very moving experience.

I remember that Queen Elizabeth II was in Canada and I read in the newspaper that she had sent her condolences to the victims and their families, and their best wishes to the injured. I waited for a handwritten Message ... (well that was long before email ... I have read in the newspaper that a similar message was sent by the Pope, but nothing came in the mail written by him either ...!!! hahaha... but the bishop did come to visit and told me about the message, some other officials of the Catholic church also visited me. Really I did not deserve any of it, I was just a common citizen, why all the attention...??

My brother Alberto, came from Germany. It had not been easy for him to find the Hospital of St. Bartholomew, asked for directions nearby and ended up in the middle of the meat market, yes, the butchers!! "Do you understand that I want the hospital and not the meat market", he asked? ... But the hospital was almost next door to the market!!!

There were no ATMs to withdraw cash in those days, the accident occurred on a Friday and Alberto received a phone call from our brother Francisco on Friday night, after the banks had closed. I had visited him often in Munich, during holidays, where Alberto studied and I had met some of his friends. He had a very nice Brazilian friend, from Rio de Janeiro, Felipe, who immediately lent him the money to travel to London. Felipe: "obrigado!!!"

Alberto phoned our mother to inform her that he had seen me, but she did not believe him, she asked to speak with me and Alberto told him I was not near a phone and I could not reached one. He explained to her that I was with a steel pin stuck through my left leg below the knee, from which hung a heavy weight at the end of the bed, the weight made the whole leg away from the hip to avoid contact with the hip to allow healing, or leaving "footprints" or "scratches" that could later become problematic.

I could not lie down because of the severe pain in the chest, but got a phone in a trolley and they wheeled it to the side of my bed, I phoned my mother in South America, she was crying, I said I was in the hospital, that I had been operated on the left leg, but she really did not believe me, she thought I had my legs amputated. The truth is that, I myself, had doubts about my situation, I could see my feet, but I could not feel my left foot and I wondered if I would get it back. One day I managed to move the left toe and my joy was enormous, if I can control a toe of that foot, surely I will get control of the others. She, my mother, Filomena, did not believe until he saw me, she travelled a few weeks after the accident, to see me in the hospital and to help me at the time I was discharged and began my recovery, walking with the aid of crutches. She was very courageous, she travelled alone, so very far, without speaking the language and without being accustomed to travel by herself, as the

My father had been traveling for vacation in Chile and it took a long time to locate him, unfortunately, he had had a stroke before and could not talk much, had difficulty walking and communicating, when he received the news of my accident, he was to about to walk down the stairs from the second floor and with the emotion, he lost his balance and fell. It took a long time for him to recover, but in his condition, it was very difficult for me to ever have a real conversation with him.

The director of my school in London, came to me in my hospital bed. "Speedy," he said, "I have more than 10,000 students at the University, and it had to be you, one of the few students I know personally," I had met him a few days earlier, at a pedestrian crossing outside of school, on the street and we talked briefly about the courses offered, the variety, the quality of the studies and the selection of subjects, I was very happy there. My course was new and he had made me some more questions, including my name, Simon, but he chose to call me "speedy" because of my Latin origin, he said, it was easier for him to remember.

The Director of Studies had already found out that I was going to be "anchored" in the hospital bed with traction and weight on the leg, over the next 45 days and would walk aided by crutches for two months and after that I would have a full recovery. He organized lecturers to go to the hospital and continue "teaching me" so I could accompany my classmates and continue my studies in the most "normal" manner as possible. They were just amazing, they were fantastic!, I was immensely impressed and eternally grateful. "Thank you all!!".

I had a nightmare, several times, staying standing still in a platform of a station of the London Underground, the crowded area, a train came and people left the train, more people boarded the train and I was left there standing, unable to move, I was alone in an empty platform when the train left and speeded away.

I have an aversion, apprehension, against crossing the tunnel Channel by train, it is a dis-comfort, not a fear, it's a "challenge" to be able to get one day closer to the "end" it is amusing, but no longer am I afraid to die, however, on the contrary, I feel prepared, there is no way of one knowing when, or where, or how it will happen, one does not choose ... ahhh ... !!! that white place ... so nice ... I invite you, it is a place worth recommending and sharing !!! All you need is to have the ticket ready...!!!

"Are you going to be worried about travelling on an underground train?" I asked Danny, my statistics professor. He continued, "You should not worry," you can continue to use the underground service, there are only two things that could happen:

a) When you use the train again, nothing may ever happen to you, so you do not have to worry about using the underground again.

b) The train may collide again, but if it did, only two things could happen: either you die and in that case you have nothing to worry about, because you'd be dead - but, if you do not die, you'll be the only person in London and the world, who has had two accidents in the underground and you would be so famous, you could write a book or make a movie, you would make a lot of money and you would not have a reason to worry", Danny was right in his reasoning!!!

The end of the tunnel? Several weeks in the hospital, unable to lie down, sit-up in bed 24 hours a day. After almost two months in the hospital, I had to walk with crutches for two months, then with the aid of a walking stick. Everything changed, I had to move from my room on the third floor to a provisional one, with no stairs and then to an apartment in the Hornsey area (residential area in North London), it was only ground floor accommodation. It was not fantastic, but fulfilled the requirements, because it was very difficult get around with crutches and do everything alone, food shopping, cleaning, laundry, ironing... it was just a room, a kitchenette that served also as dining area and a shared bathroom with other students.

Ahhh, very important, I had access to a garden, for my exclusive use ... yes it was a luxury in London ... the winter was very cold and as I had to wash my own clothes, one day, I hung up on the patio my favourite shirt, a black shirt, to dry outdoors, but I forgot and the following morning, I saw it outside, hanging in the same place where I had hung it, but it was hard, all rigid as if starched and I thought for a moment, "ohhh...no !!! my favourite shirt is going to break into pieces as if made of glass!!!... I immediately burst out laughing ... I really woke up and thought," How will break???, it is only frozen, the ice melts quickly and there!! No problem...!!! lol...

The lawyers came to make a claim against the organization that administered the London underground in those days. They helped to get the money for my mother's trip from South America to London, to cover all your expenses, among other things.

I was traveling as it was common among many of the students at the time in London, trying to save a few pennies on the underground journey when attending classes. I had bought a ticket to enter the metro and then handed a coin to the station guard at the destination's exit and that was the situation the day of the accident. I had not purchased the ticket for the entire journey, lol!!! ... I was very worried I had done something wrong!!, I told my lawyer exactly what happened, he reassured me telling me that it was not relevant, the fact was that the train had crashed, I had been injured, I could have died and the legal process was clear in my defence, despite not having purchased my "full fare" ticket.

Today I say that one has to make sure, during one's lifetime, to have your "ticket" the "entrance ticket" into heaven, the ticket to eternity, at the time that one would have to depart for the eternal life and not have to be "thrown" into hell. I know very clearly where and how to get that "ticket" to go there and not have to "return", or having to go first to another destination, the undesirable...!!

There were several theories about the cause of the accident, including one that the driver had been drinking alcohol, but he did not drink, his colleagues saw him very well that morning and in the post-mortem tests, it could not be categorically established whether he had been drinking alcohol. He could also have been "daydreaming" or falling asleep while driving the train, but the sharp movement prior to the impact should have made him protect his face, however, the driver was found in the normal operating position, without having tried to protect himself. There were those who argued that had he committed suicide, but he had in his pocket £300 that he would use that day to buy a car for his daughter, after work, making it very unlikely that he would have killed himself committing suicide.

Another argument was that he could have been distracted and thought Moorgate station was closed and had to go on to the next one, without realizing that this was the last station and he just accelerated to arrive quickly to the next station, the fact that there was a slope down, made it easier to accelerate. There were comments from other colleagues of the deceased driver, that this was a very boring route, very short and to lose concentration for a few seconds and feel the movement of the train before entering the station, then to see the platform, he probably thought, better to go on to the next station, as it was too late to stop at this station and did not realize that was the last station on the route and the tunnel did not continue, there was nothing that would make him remember that this was the last station or warned him of the danger of continuing. I am of the opinion that this was the correct explanation of what happened that day. I have read that currently Moorgate station is "haunted", the reason of the crash remains a mystery.

There was no time, no time frame, no "past", "present" or "future", from the moment of the accident, time really ceased to exist, from the moment of the impact of the train against the wall at the end of the tunnel and my departure to earthly life, I visited the heavens (or whatever you call the place of eternal good), and then experienced visiting hell (or whatever you want your name the place of eternal punishment), I had no notion of time, everything could have happened in five minutes, but in reality it was nearly five hours...!!!

You cannot imagine how hard it is for me to believe what happened and I imagine how difficult it must be for you to believe what I'm telling you, I want to record my experiences, feelings, as they were and as I remember them.

I have described here the facts, how eventually I heard the rescuers ... I was rescued ... I believe it was not me, but were guardian angels who helped me, because I was not aware of what was happening from the moment of impact, I "switched off" I had no reason to respond to the call, to the question "is there anybody else there?" I was guided in my actions, you know?, that is a fact, being in eternity is like falling asleep and you have no sense of time and one does not act "knowingly", I would not have had a reason to ask for help or to reply, if it had not been with a "little help"...

Born again?, really anyone that "is brought back" to this life, do it for different reasons and with different goals in different circumstances. You ever seen a fish out of the water?, was caught by someone, but then returned to the sea, some bleeding, others unscathed, they are different experiences for different fish ... they are very different experiences for us ... we are all different, we can go through situations that may be similar, but basically they are very different and there is no single right way, only to make sure you have the correct ticket to eternal life, when you get to hear "is there anybody else there???"...

What do Moses, Napoleon, John F. Kennedy, Mother Teresa of Calcutta, your great-great-grandparents or great-great-grandmothers, Hitler and Pope John Paul II have in common? They're all dead, no matter what they did, the money they managed to put together or the works they did, they have all passed into eternal life. They endure in eternity, everyone did something different and none of them managed to paint the "Mona Lisa", but they will not be remembered, nor judged by the paintings they did or did not do, but by what they did in their surroundings and environment.

We must agree that we cannot all be "miss universe", or the best soccer player of the year, nor remain in those positions throughout all of your life, it's similar to being in a the supermarket, you see many things, we imagine others, dream, have hopes, expectations, have the option to choose between one or more alternatives, but then after having made our decisions, at the end we have to "pay the bill", regardless of whether the selections were good or bad. Simon ... you understand? If you want you can pay your bill in advance or at the time of going through the "till" or sign the credit card and pay in instalments, but no one escapes having to pay the bills...

SECOND PART

12
After Moorgate

Life changed for me. There was a "before" and an "after" Moorgate. I've heard other people talk about a "before and after Christ," that is, people with similar experiences to mine. I used to be a "normal" person, with nothing unusual happening in my life, but after Moorgate, life was full of interesting, intense and unusual events. My luck also changed from "normal" to "very good" extremely abnormal and unpredictable, with very extreme and powerful events. I stopped being concerned about life and about dying, no longer bothered me the possibility of dying. Dying to me now is just another "chapter" in life, another form of existence, as one might be eating, sleeping, swimming and could also be in the state of "dead", as another form of existence. I feel I've been there, in the "dead" state and have returned to earthly life. Common situations for me now are falling asleep whilst floating on the water, at sea or in a swimming pool, or even falling asleep in the dentist's chair while working on my teeth...!!!

I have never been back at the same platform at Moorgate station, in fact I've never seen any of the television images of the train crash at Moorgate, since there was no TV in the hospital room and had no video to watch after leaving hospital. Events were recorded in my "hard disk" on the top of my head, but there are still many unanswered questions: why I survived and the woman sitting opposite me had to die? Why have I come back?, why have I been given another chance? What is the real mission I have to complete?

I did not feel any closer to God, I did not feel closer to any religion after the Moorgate event, in fact, it was the opposite. I had not done anything to deserve the "second chance", but the "second chance" really was something that I did not understand in its full extent, until many years later, I had the wrong concept, we could say "materialistic", time taught me and showed me the right way ... do you understand Simon? Really at the end, at the "exit", life will show you the bill for everything and if you have enough credits, you will enjoy what you have sown...

13
The New South America For Investment

I had the chance to give some talks in London, on how to do business in Latin America and in them, I referred to an experience I had with Stephanie, an Australian girlfriend I had in my time as a student in London, she always wanted me to tell her how life was in South America, Chile, Peru, Brazil and elsewhere, and of course, I did tell her about different customs and information on these countries. I explained to my audiences, for example, how had told Stephanie about Santiago and the Mapocho river, how the big ships laden with goods from Europe arrived there, bringing all the fresh fish, which was sold directly on the market in the city centre, which was located very near the port of the Mapocho river, the boats were loaded there with many types of bananas, tropical jungle fruits, sugar and the coal extracted from mines located in the deserts of Chile, near Santiago.

I would tell Stephanie about Lima, that I had heard that they had opened recently a new international airport in 1980 and that was the first concrete building in the city and also, it had three floors, was the tallest building in the city ...!!! Lima was very poor, where most of the houses were wooden buildings of one or two floors only and still people mainly circulated through the streets on horseback. Lima was already a very large city with about 80,000 inhabitants, living mainly from agriculture and mining. The port of Lima was large and receiving vessels at least once a month, coming from Europe and sailed up the Rímac River, to the city of Huancayo, where they loaded the minerals which were transported to Europe. Lima is a city where only rains at night, this helped keeping the mountains with permanent snow around the city.

I continued explaining Stephanie that Brazil had two major cities, one was Rio de Janeiro, where two large beaches, with pure sand and very warm and calm sea were benefited with a constant summer, the sun shines all year, Rio is a paradise that had a lot of vegetation, natural pine and eucalyptus trees, the city was very quiet, no industry is allowed, to maintain a beautiful and unpolluted climate. Rio was very cheerful, friendly and only with affluent people, the transport system is free and had a very efficient subway that goes directly to the beaches from all the residential areas.

I explained to my audiences, that I would tell Stephanie that one of my favourite cities was Bogotá with nice views to the Caribbean beaches, unrivalled, some had very calm warm waters and with very few visitors, other beaches had very cold water and rocky shores, all were fantastic, clean and very secure, Bogotá was very advanced and modern, surrounded by sand dunes and from this city started a train offering a tour around the country, crossing the Andes through many tunnels, reaching villages located at 5300 meters above sea level and then across the Amazon rainforest with many bridges, some of them very high, allowing the passage of cargo ships below. This journey was made in the same train and lasted seven days to give the entire tour around Colombia. In each town on the route, the Government provided money to all those who wished to build industries and start farms, so that there was many people from various countries coming and opening businesses that generated many jobs. It was very easy to make the tour of Colombia, as there was always a train departing every four hours, they all made this complete journey.

My speeches to bankers, investors and business people in London were to explain with irony, why they should be interested in doing business with Latin America in general, the goal of my talks was to convince listeners that they had to visit those countries, the entire region see with their own eyes, because what you hear, is not necessarily true, there were great opportunities, but not all that glitters is gold. What happened to Stephanie, when I said that really the Mapocho and Rimac rivers were not navigable, nor could any ships sail from the sea, up to levels above 3000 meters above sea level etc. was that...
 I never saw Stephanie again, but if someone was really interested in doing business with Latin America, they'd best travel and visit personally, there were

some things that were true, but they should discover for themselves.

Of course all this happened before access to the internet, where you can quickly verify the information you receive, but still, you cannot believe everything so easily, you can hang any information, retouched photos ...., and the best football games of the world championship in Haiti in 2001!!! ...You can date someone who hung a picture as a teenager in the belief that the person still has the same "look" ... Some things are true, but one has to decide what things to believe, it is oneself that decides on what to have faith.

I accept criticism, how easy it is to convince others, especially of what the others don't know and when they believe that you are telling the truth, in reality, those are temptations of mockery, temptations handled by those who dominate the "hot place", where the horrible screams are and I already visited and do not want to go back, being full of ostentation, selfishness, self-praise, is also a wish of that "club" and the more I think about it, the more I think the other "club" is better and I am convinced that we must be prepared with the right ticket to go there in the right moment ...

My talks in London included explanations of all that development which was possible in South America, although much of that money was not actually spent on the projects of development by the same governments, but schemes were setup deviate the funds legally away from the States, companies were opened by the rulers themselves and their friends, they did a lot of publicity for the governments, spending really amazingly large amounts of money, it is very easy to control how many bricks go into a building and then find out the right cost of the bricks to get to know the real cost of a project, while in advertising, you can spend lots of money and no one can say that the amount of many millions is not justified for a health campaign, feeding the hungry, or in education. Whether the projects are built or not cannot be controlled in the advertising industry and no one can criticize. That advertising money can easily be used for the press to support governments, as each company radio, television or newspapers that do not support the Governments, loses advertising and therefore give-up the easy money ... hmmm ... that sounds like a good deal, right?

Of course, if you want to be sarcastic you can say that the system is very good, in that way more entrepreneurs who can make new investments are created and thus make the economy grow in these Countries, and why not? You may then tell me, because that money is mine...!!! Well, it wasn't it you that chose that government? And if the controllers, the lawmakers disagree, you can always give them some money, or twice the amount, or give them more, to vote in favour of the government, have you not heard that everyone has a price?... those are things of this world, the imperfections of man (and woman...hahaha... here is no escaping for them... hahaha) really all our actions are those that feed our soul and if we let greed, hatred, revenge, resentment, lies, rampage to guide us, without a doubt, our souls will be damaged and then suffer the consequences, remember ?

Generally the mother expecting a child, does not get drunk or do drugs, or make outrageous things, because she cares for her child and wants the child to have the best possibilities in life, it's the same with your soul, in life I believe we should take care, feed it, give it all the nourishment you can and if you ask me and how I do that? Telling the truth, taking care of whoever is close to you, truly loving and above all avoiding idolatry...what? Idolatry???...what??, are you crazy? You may say that idolatry no longer exists, that is something from the past ...Right?, the desire to accumulate money or accumulating (and consuming), overeating (including chocolates !!!), or to always want the latest cell phone (or maybe lipsticks...), or prefer to watch a football game instead of talking and listen to your children, friends or family? or to love your partner too much, any of these things can create idolatry, no one told you that ?, ask yourself if your God receives equal attention, roughly more or less?, remember they all are "brownie points" counting towards your ticket to that place of the white light...

Talking someone into believing ...is a temptation... I remember the time I flew, I will not say with whom, or where, but it was the first time the other person, who sat next to me, was traveling by plane, I gave him the window seat and after a few minutes I told him that always the same images were shown on every flight, as the film that was projected in all the "windows" of the aircraft, were the same in all aircraft... I laughed for a moment, but then I felt bad ... well it was not fair to make fun of someone's innocence...

Or perhaps the time the little mouse got into the house and we locked in someone, I will not say whom or where...I will only say that it was in the main bathroom of the house, where we heard screams, banging...and we just laughed...

Ahh, I remember that we invited a foreign couple to have dinner with us, as we knew them a long time... bahhh it was less than twelve months later that we met again and they were very thankful of the dinner we prepared for them... dinner, dinner?, what dinner? Carolina and I asked each other, but you prepared a paella for us and it was delicious and we sat together by the fireplace, eating some red berries ice cream ... Carolina looked at me and I looked at her, but both with such ignorance of the facts ... how could it be possible that we both had erased from our minds that dinner? The truth, the truth is that until today, I do not understand how we could both have fully forgotten about that event, or was it that it never happened?? ... hahaha... Simon does not understand this time...!!!

It also happened that the boy, the son of a neighbour, Jaime shouted during mealtime, "someone is stealing the TV"!!!, we all continued eating ... "they are stealing the TV !!!". .shouted the boy ... when we finished eating ... oops!!! Someone had stolen the TV...!!!

14
Carlos The Jackal

Walking down the street with shopping bags hanging from the handles of the crutches, now living in a different part of London. One day I opened the front door of the house, there were two men in dark suits who had rung the bell and said they were nothing less than of the "Scotland Yard" (Police detectives at my door...???) and they wanted to talk to me. "Sure," I said, "Please go ahead, come in" and as they were walking into the house, I said, "by the way, I'm not Carlos," they both stopped worried and asked me "how do you know, we came to see you about that" they asked, "easy, I've done nothing wrong and some people have already told me that there is a resemblance between Carlos the Jackal" and I".

The Jackal was a political terrorist, kidnapper, Venezuelan of the 1970's, who at the time was one of the most sought after fugitives in the world, now a prisoner (with a life sentence in France). The guys from Scotland Yard started to relax a bit, then I showed him my passport and they compared the picture with one of Carlos the Jackal and they said, "don't they look alike?", I said "no", "but if you show me the picture of two Chinese people, surely they will look alike". They asked me why I was on crutches?, after hearing my answer and as I told them the story of my accident on the train, they were convinced that they were following the wrong man ...!!! Although many times I travelled through Paris and then read in the newspapers that "Carlos the Jackal, had been seen in Paris" ... sometimes traveling through Germany, Italy, England and often seemed funny to see sometimes uniformed police following me through the streets... sometimes I saw detectives, waiting for me outside a restaurant and then follow me... hahaha... for me it was thoroughly funny...!!!

15
Astral Travel – The Abduction

Several times, during the night, while sleeping, I felt my bed rise, losing contact with the floor and floated in the middle of my room, I realized I had my hands up at shoulder level, under the quilt and needed only to stretch an arm to turn on the light in the room. I could not move, I knew I had to have light to make sure what happened, but then, my bed went to the window of the room and went through it, floating through the space and then returning by the same route, but I could not move. When the bed stopped moving, I turned on the light and checked that it was in the same place. Fear?, no, I really was just unable to move, I was "frozen", as the image of the TV.

Another night, I woke up and I moved my arms, I managed to elevate from the bed, first lying on my back and then standing up and also lying on my chest, I went out the window, flying through the trees, but I thought, I wondered was I really awake?, or perhaps it's no more than a dream?, I carefully observed the way I was moving my arms, I had to learn how to repeat that movement at will. I never repeated the trip exactly under my own will, I repeated it itself several times, at night, during my "sleep"?, I thought, ahh

... I know how to move the arms in order to be able to fly, but I've never managed to fly, whilst being fully "awake", it is curious that I do make other flights going to different locations, sometimes premeditating the place I want to visit, or visiting people whom I want to see, sometimes I just fly through unknown places. Would this have a relation to the abduction? ... What??? !!!, yes, abduction !!!".

A night with a full moon, the day before a lunar eclipse, I was with Carolina leaving a supermarket in Brazil, pushing the shopping trolley in the car park, something made us to look at the sky, it was so clear and beautiful, no wind, there was a very pleasant temperature and light breeze. Suddenly some lights appeared in the sky, to the south an object was the sky, the object appeared dark, but with different coloured flashing lights, turning on and off in a certain sequence. A UFO!!!, we shouted together at the same time. The UFO began to move north, but then fell, rose, paused, it looked as if it was signalling with the lights and then it quickly rose further and disappeared, as if it had "switched off" the lights. We were astonished at the sight, neither of us had ever seen a UFO, nor had we anticipated that we would see one. It was "awesome", exciting, intriguing, we were not frightened, nor did it cause any discomfort, we rather had a sense of satisfaction, having both seen it, something so different, so clear, rare and strange at the same time.

One day when Carolina was alone in Brazil, I had travelled to Buenos Aires for two days, Carolina was with a Brazilian friend, Giana, when suddenly Carolina felt on her left arm a sensation, as if an insect was walking under the skin, she was frightened, but there was nothing on the skin, it was under her skin!! !, there was a hard and rigid object, it was about half a centimetre long and looked round, cylindrical, like a grain of rice. The object was moving rapidly, down her arm, under the skin, to just below the elbow. "Carolinaaaa, what is that?" Giana wondered. "I do not know ..." replied Carolina and they both went to see a doctor at the hospital, "no, sorry we do not see these cases here," they went to another hospital where eventually she was seen, does it hurt?, do you feel any discomfort?, not, ok good, they said, please use this cream and it should go away within a week...

The next day I returned from Argentina and I saw a little above her left wrist at the back, a hard object, under the skin, just like the size of a grain of rice, what could it be?, here was no pain, no itching or rash, or other symptoms. She told me how the object had moved under the skin of her arm, there was no visible sign of cutting or that there had been a splinter or anything in her arm. I pressed it with my nails and was very hard, we knew it was there, but did not know what it was. We observed it and in two days, it could not be seen again, she did not feel it anymore. Had it "disappeared"?

After several months, we saw a report on television about people who had seen UFOs and had seen some combination of lights flashing, like signals. Ahh...we thought, would that have anything to do with our experience in Brazil?... the report indicated that several of these people, later had been abducted ... huyyyy !!! ... would this be possible? We saw the UFO, the lights... What would this...? Announcement of an abduct...?, Hummm ...

A short while after, we saw a documentary on television about an American surgeon (Dr. Roger Leir), a doctor who had located several people with objects that had suddenly appeared under the skin, without any surgery or implant marks, he had then extracted surgery several of those objects, which were precisely the size of a grain of rice ... !!!. The extracted objects were radio wave transmitters, they have been analysed by several American laboratories and described as made of metals that are not present on the surface of the earth, but in the centre of the earth and in meteorites, they are said to contain elements of nanotechnology...., the objects or implants do not cause pain or are uncomfortable, they can be located under the skin of the arms or legs, surrounded by nerves....that seemed to be a description of what we saw happen with Carolina ... ??? !!! ? Gulp!!!...

Some people reported that they were abducted and then they had perceived the implanted objects!!... oops!!!, that has also happened to me!!!, I remember that I also had the experience of being awakened from my sleep and be taken, floating into a ship (UFO) which moved very fast, I was taken to a place where they had other people, it was a kind of a temple, where there was a ceremony in which all were participating, I can only describe it as very nice, comforting and I have no more memories, I have no notion for time there either, then we went back on the ship (UFO) that left us back in our hometowns ... what ??? I thought this is very easy, there are only two possibilities, may be all of it is true or it is not, but really it does not matter to us either way, therefore, we can continue our normal life and consider it as a new extreme experience, additional to many that are reported here and like many others that I am leaving out, but nevertheless, are all true. My goal remains the same, to be prepared with the ticket that allows me to return to the white light I have seen and I long to return to her.

16
The Flights From New York

My plane took off from New York, bound for London, it felt "heavy", "jumbo" two-story planes are always heavy, the plane continued slowly, but it was still very low, I had a feeling that it already should be climbing more and the notice to fasten seat belts should not be turned off ?, "ding !!" ... this is the aircraft commander, I have to tell you that there has been a small problem, a window of the cockpit has opened and we cannot close it, because of the pressure, so we have to return to the airport in New York, but before that we will fly very low for about an hour and you will see a "spray" coming out of the tips of the wings, that is the fuel that we need to dump before we are able to return to the airport, for safety reasons, during all that time: PLEASE DO NOT SMOKE OR LIGHT A MATCH OR LIGHTER OR ANYTHING SIMILAR !!!

After all that time flying very low and largely passengers keeping silent on the plane, all staring at each other, there was a message again, fasten your seat belts and we are going to land, like in the movies, police cars, fire engines, ambulances could be seen, flashing lights on either side of the plane, as we landed. Fortunately everything run smoothly, we left the plane and as it was very late, we stayed in hotels overnight and continued our journey the next day, without any problems.

My plane took off from New York, bound for London, it felt "heavy", "jumbo" two-story planes are always heavy, the plane continued slowly, but it was still very low, I had a feeling that it already should be climbing more and the notice to fasten seat belts should not be turned off?, "ding !!" ... this is the aircraft commander, I have to tell you that there has been a small problem... What??? I have already been through this chapter...or am I wrong?...we have an indicator light on the operation panel, which indicates that the landing gear is not fully retracted as it should be... so we have to return to the airport in New York, but before that we will fly very low for about an hour and you will see a "spray" coming out of the tips of the wings, that is the fuel that we need to dump before we are able to return to the airport, for safety reasons, during all that time: PLEASE DO NOT SMOKE OR LIGHT A MATCH OR LIGHTER OR ANYTHING SIMILAR !!! ahhh ... the movie was not the same but very similar !!! That was boring!!! I settled in my seat ... and fell asleep. Ding!!! I woke to the announcement to fasten your seat belts, we are going to land, and how does he know? That man who sits on the nose of the plane, on the second floor, if the landing gear is now in place to land??..., I wondered if something has already failed, could it now give the correct information, that the landing gear is in the correct place?...uuuyyy!!!, I was worried and then I calmed down, I remembered that you have to have Faith ... !!!

17
And The Fire At The Hotel?

Having been to Cuba and Mexico, I was with summer clothes when I had to make a stopover in New York, I had to spend the night in a hotel near the airport to make a connecting flight, before travelling to another of the Caribbean islands, again early the next morning. It was winter and there was snow in New York, but was very tired and went to sleep early also had to get up very early to continue the journey. I thought I heard a buzzer or alarm, but it stopped and I went back to sleep, the alarm sounded again, this time I heard it more intense and turned on the light in the room, there was a very large bell, about 30 centimetres in diameter that was ringing inside my room, but happily it stopped ringing. When I was about to turn off the light, the alarm sounded again and now, I was awake and heard it very clearly and very loud. I thought, ahhh, these "gringos", how inconsiderate to test the fire alarm at this time ... oops!! And what if it is not a test? I thought ...?, As the noise was unbearable, I went to the door of my room and looked through the "magic eye" I just saw a hotel employee who raised the internal phone it was next to the elevator in front of my room and I heard him say: "on this floor there is also a lot of smoke, I will go to the floor above to see and will let you know"... ohhhh...

I stuck my nose close to the edge of the door and sensed a burning smell... Uuuyyy !! ...I looked for some clothes very quickly and opened the door, it was true, to the right side of the corridor it was quite smoky, but to the left side there was no smoke and at the end of the corridor the emergency escape door was open and all the hotel guests were walking down the fire escape on the outside of the building, pyjamas, coats, anything, it was half past one in the morning!!! And it was snowing!!! ... So I followed the people going down the emergency stair and we were all outside the hotel in the cold for a few minutes and then we were allowed to enter the reception area of the hotel. The vast majority of us were more concerned about getting to sleep, than by the fire and so, after nearly an hour, the fire chief said we could return to our rooms and continue "back to normal", we all hurried back, as we were informed that there had only been a small fire on the 3rd floor and I went back to sleep in my room located on the fifth floor. Do you understand Simon?, one day you will definitely go for ever, you will go, just as when you arrived, without anything material and everything will continue...and what was recorded on the "chip" you received at birth, you transmitted "modified" to your children and what you recorded in the "chip" they received are your qualities of art, music, love of your neighbour, math skills or maybe teaching. This is also recorded in the "historical" in your life and is the "energy" that your own soul will use and will indicate the direction that it will have. Simon, there are signals that indicate to you, not follow this path and you don't pay any attention... do you understand Simon?? Anytime you'll be leaving your body on earth and your soul will continue, it will be your decision where it will go!!!

18
Life In Brazil

Being among various clients in Sao Paulo, Brazil, visiting large companies and being with people that had a lot of money, I learned a lot about life in Brazil, their races, their joy of life, their customs, values and I even learned Portuguese. I was invited to spend a weekend at the home of Robert, a major customer, of European origin. Robert had lots of money and enjoyed to "live well", his house was by a lake, had a swimming pool, sports courts and even a jetty with a boat to sail around and to go fishing in the lake. We had beer, caipirinha (typical Brazilian alcoholic beverage, made of a sugar cane alcoholic beverage and lemon), lots of barbequed meat at the grill, plenty of sunshine and the guests began to arrive, other important business people related to Robert, most of the guests were between 40 and 50 years of age.

It was very hot, the sun was stronger around noon and I was by the pool, so I decided to go back to my room, to find the sun protection lotion, to avoid having to regret later with skin burns. When I entered my room I was surprised to see a girl, brunette about 18 years old, in my room, completely naked and smiling, she had a very beautiful body, she was slim, long black hair, I then thought very quickly, who this girl could be, she really looked so good... Was she the daughter of one of these entrepreneurs?, would she be someone's partner?, what should I say?, what should I do? Why was she in my room and ... completely naked?, I reciprocated her smile and didn't consider it proper to just leave the room, I thought it was better to act perfectly normal, so I said "olá bom day !!" ("hi"), she smiled again and I continued looking for my sun lotion, so she also carried on, she went into the bathroom and sat down, without closing the door, I heard the sound of liquid... and when I found my bronzer, I just said "thank you" and left the room, returning to the pool, but then I realized that this "thank you" had a "double meaning"...hahaha...

I told Robert about my experience and he said that she was the new18 year old wife of Joseph, his best friend who had just turned 50 years old... !!!, "Welcome to Brazil"!!!

There were several situations of "temptation", Robert invited girlfriends and sometimes other girls, "strangers", but I did not see that with good eyes, the idea that I could turn "addicted, dependent" due to the invitations from my client, thinking of my carnal pleasure, even worse, if it was controlled by someone else....This was not in accordance with my ideas or beliefs, one can get close to fire for heat, but if you get too close, it burns!!!, if one continues, you get scorched or you could feel too cold when you get away from the fire... warm water is more enjoyable than the very hot or the very cold water, I learned that the "balance" is best. Some may come to the edge of the cliff, watching and observing, but others do not come close, for the fear of falling.

Strange things happen in life and Frank, my European partner saw the opportunity to connect directly with Robert, without my knowledge. Robert organized a party in Brazil, let's say a "carnival" where everything was allowed, he spent a large amount of money and hired an entire nightclub, only for themselves. I realized that, this was what Robert wanted to do with me. Frank was amazed at such a novel way of doing business and also getting himself such great pleasures at the same time. He took on the business alone, leaving me on the side-line without recognizing my efforts financially, of course, in reality, what Frank wanted was to have the benefit of the pleasures more than the business, well, both things were "tied" to each other.
I defended what I thought was the right thing, defending what my "principles" indicated was right, we had to enter into a long legal process to determine responsibilities, still I felt that my partner had violated my rights, had taken advantage of my work, I felt I had lost everything material that I had obtained. The boss, based in Germany was Otto, Frank blatantly lied to Otto, reporting fictitious clients visits, he had supposedly made, on days that actually were holidays, reporting non-existent meetings. Eventually, Otto acknowledged that he had been deceived, it was a very difficult situation for everyone.

I lost a lot of my health, tranquillity at home, I lost a lot of time, I gained a lot of earthly experience. With the final stage of negotiation, I was in shock, which lasted for about a week, I could not absorb the fact that people in whom I had confidence, could fail to recognize contracts, promises and commitments that were documented.

In the end much of the struggle was for money, the principles were "negotiated" and the agreements were "adapted", regardless of the truth, in favour of convenience. My understanding of the "values" of life were broken again and I could not do anything about it, the shock was tremendous. Again, I found that firms act directed human beings, governed by economic or political interests, there are judges who are easily corrupted and show examples that are not worthy of imitation. The true God is replaced by the god called "money". Again it was very clear to me and saw that the Ombudsman, politicians, they back the interests of created groups or institutions with large capitals, where the objectives are to favour specific groups. Advertising purchases support within the media, it is the materialism in the world, it is a modern form of "idolatry" purely trivial, temporary, finite, we can say that guided by the "evil chief" that has to create those many temptations that attract and trap many. I admit I've been tempted many times and have been on the "brink" of the abyss, I have been able to observe and go back in time, without falling off the cliff. Uggh!!!, how difficult and dangerous that is... !!! not recommend!!!, is smarter to learn from the experience of others, it's about having Faith !!!, you know Simon ... ???, nobody is perfect ... !!! Simon, take care!!! You can fall off the cliff Simon!!!

I had an economic gain as a result of these events or negotiations but I respected without discussion, the agreements I had made. I did not ask myself whether that was important, to me it was obvious to respect the word, even if one stands to suffered material losses. What does it mean to be a "winner" of a confrontation?, can pride be so strong ?, is that selfishness can give so much satisfaction?

Having some kind of material success, could be seen as the player of a third division, who is recognized, he had to fight hard and then is taken to the second division, where he has to start all over again and fight and be recognized once again, only to be led to the first division, receiving more demands and fight all over again. What do we learn?, that each one of us is different and we have different requirements at every stage of your life things become ever more demanding, there are increasing demands, as we go along the path of life and cannot pretend to be equal to this or that person. We know that even a Saint is very different from other Saint and there is no magic formula that will make one attain a particular position, each one of us develops their own future. These "winners" or Saints are those who have managed to administer their abilities or human qualities, so that their souls, "connected" in eternal life, are able to give further help to others in the transitional stage of life. Those are some of the important things of our earthly life. Simon ... do you understand Simon?

Driving through really nice places in Brazil, along with Carolina, where there are many very nice beaches, lots of vegetation, clean air, breath-taking scenery, rivers, streams, valleys, different climates, rain, ice, sun, dry weather and wet weather. At one place on the top of a hill, we decided to stop to see a fantastic valley bordering the hills, with a river at the bottom of the valley, truly one of those heavenly places. We thought it would be nice to spend a few days in that peaceful and stunning location. We were told by one person of another place that was even more attractive than that, there was a lookout point, a hotel that was under construction, but then it was abandoned and she gave us directions on how to get there, she was a native speaker who stood out from all others, being the only Brazilian whom we have known that was not smiling...!!!

After driving about 10km in the direction where the brunette had indicated, we asked the village people about the location of the Montes Nevados hotel we had been indicated, as we wanted to get to the lookout point, strangely nobody wanted to acknowledge its existence or its location, given that we were only 600 metres away. We choose to follow our own sense of direction, based on the explanation that we originally received and arrived via a dirt track to the entrance of the Hotel Montes Nevados. Then we had to drive another 100 meters inside the property to get to the main hotel building, it was more like a country house and standing at the door was a woman, with African features, it looked like she had been waiting for us, she welcomed us, we asked her to do a tour of the hotel, there was a strong smell of damp, the beds were not made, they seemed almost abandoned. There was not a single host, or any other employee, only the black woman, whom looked as if extracted from a novel of the history of African immigrants to Brazil.

We did not feel comfortable being there, there was a strange atmosphere, it was not appealing, so finally we asked the hostess for directions to reach the lookout point we wanted and that was that just 3 minutes in the car, following the dirt road, the same that we had taken to get to that place we were on the right track and it seemed odd that no one wanted to give us any help to find it. Along the way, my wife yawned aloud, and said that she was very sleepy but how are you going to sleep now we've been looking for this place...?, the viewpoint, we're almost there ... I said don't sleep now..., she answered, yawning and almost falling asleep...I am very tired... Here...!!!, we... !!! ... look!!! Carolina!!!, there was an abandoned, neglected building, with plants, spaces for windows, but without them, the paint was dirty with black mould, nobody around, it was a truly creepy atmosphere!!!

Let's get out! Carolina said, trying to open the door and waking up...!!! Are you crazy!!!???, you are not getting out !!!, I pulled her by her arm, closing the door and speeding away ... but we wanted to see the view of the valley !!!, we should go to the lookout point!! I repeated: NO, you are NOT getting out here!! IShe asked but why not??, this place scares me and I drove quickly to get to another town, where we decided to stay overnight in a large, new and comfortable hotel !!! There, we saw an ad for "Reiki" home service, a service that for some time we had heard of and wanted to try out, we wanted to experience how would that alternative medicine worked, healing by imposing hands, without touching the body.

A new experience, Ana came to the hotel, a girl who told us a little of her role and asked if we were tourists, sightseeing and what places we had visited. We told her about the experience of the beautiful valley, the Hotel and Montes Nevados and the creepy place we saw, without being able to reach the viewpoint. Whaaatt???, did you really get there ?, Ana rebuked us, did you feel sleepy there ?, well, Carolina did feel very tired and sleepy, just as we were arriving and gave Ana more details. Carolina had been falling into "a vacuum", relaxing because she felt suddenly she was losing her energy, but she felt that the place attracted her at the same time, part of her inner self felt more vigilant. With some care, Ana explained that there was really was such a viewpoint, but it was a point of "negative energy" around where sacrifices, voodoo, black magic and other strange things happened, that was not a place where we should go!!! that place was kept "secret" to avoid scaring tourism in the region. That was our first experience of healing and alternative medicine, positive energy (reiki) and the existence of negative energy in that strange place. Simon ... really, you see that the power of evil really exists and is very powerful ?, the devil is the king of evil, the devil dominates certain areas, people and is always looking to attract more "curious" or "naive" ...Simón... Simon ... when will you learn ...? Beware Simon!!! And take care of Carolina!!

Two years later, Cleide, a Brazilian friend, told us that her brother Joao and his girlfriend Daisy were travelling around in the area of the hotel Montes Nevados, but did not get any hotel rooms available in the region, only in the same Montes Nevados was a room available, so they spent the night there and it was very nice, although they were the only guests in the hotel. At breakfast they ate a mushroom omelette that was outstanding and asked the hostess, that black woman we had met, if she had prepared it with local ingredients, the lady replied with a smile, yes they are local ingredients and very fresh, the Gnomes harvested the mushrooms this morning ... !!!! Joao and Daysi and told of their experiences to Cleide and she was very surprised, it was then that she told them about our experience.... hummmm... that is nerve-wracking !!! exclaimed Daysi...

We lived with my wife Carolina for a long time in Brazil, we had heard stories of people that had been burgled, even whilst they were in their own homes, houses, condos and even apartment buildings. We were very careful. We had just rented a very comfortable, modern apartment with sea view on the tenth floor, had three bedrooms, two bathrooms, living room, kitchen and we were sleeping there one night when I heard a noise, followed by steps of a person walking slowly on the wooden floor, I could hear the footsteps getting closer to our bedroom and then the door of our bedroom started to open, "AAAHHHH ...!!!"I yelled, raising the bed cover and throwing it at the door while getting out of bed and I heard someone, a female voice screaming "aaaaaa!!!" Carolina was returning from the kitchen after having drunk some water, our loud screams, followed by laughter, surely would have generated concern among neighbours, why are these people making such a noise during the night...??? ... hahaha... !!!

After the train accident, my behaviour was similar to that of the politician who suddenly emerges and becomes known, as the artist who overnight becomes the attraction, who is "lost" in their new "status", does not have time to devote to each event, each person, as it merits. A brain that thinks he's always deserved success and attention, a brain that thinks for itself on being the centre of the universe, not of the whole universe, where it is just a "small dot", as important as all the others who are around and that are far too selfish !! Simon ..., you have said it !!!

19
Karen And Alberto Passed Away

I remember Karen travelled by train from Scotland to London to visit me in the hospital, like many others, but she did not receive the recognition she deserved, the attention she deserved for her closeness, her friendship so special we had, I kept her distant. she had to "queue" like everyone else and I did not value the effort she had made to visit me, having travelled long hours by train, was perhaps her "obligation" to make the trip to visit me? That was the last time I saw Karen and soon after, no one saw her again, I learned that he had died, she hanged herself in her apartment, what was the motive that led her to commit suicide?, only then I stopped to think about her, his qualities, the energy that was felt around her, we will never know her final thoughts, each of us is a book of experiences and no follows exactly the same route, or react in the same way to the same stimuli, Simon you don't understand?, you don't learn ?, do you need more signs?

Seven months later, I lost my brother Alberto, he died of a stomach disease, the day and at the time I was in an airplane, when we had just started to descend to Paris airport in France. I felt his "presence", hard to explain, but as you feel the smell of a flower and recognize what it is or feel the sound of the waves and you know it's the sea, I felt his "presence" and when I heard of his death, I was surprised that his death was just when I had felt that strange feeling, let's say he appeared to be saying "goodbye", we had prayed together recently, he had a stomach problem, it was inoperable, we wanted to keep in touch and work together, I did not abandon him and he has not abandoned me either, Alberto helps me to this day. I confirmed that money is worthless, it means nothing when one dies, there are other more important things, more valuable resources in the end, happiness in eternal life is what matters.

20
Nalda

A Brazilian friend, Anelis, told us about her experience of having contacted a lady, well known in political circles in Brazil, Dra. Nalda, that by reading tarot cards, could see the future very accurately and she had been very successful with her travel, friendships and family relationships. Carolina and I had several extreme experiences some negative things in our lives that had happened to us recently and we wanted to have an idea, to know more details of whether these radical experiences would continue for long. Carolina obtained an appointment to see Dr. Nalda, but she warned that she only saw women. I took my wife to Nalda's apartment and she would call me when they would finish, to pick her up, but I had only driven about one kilometre in the car after leaving, when Carolina called me and told me: "come back", what happened?, I asked and he said he Nalda began to read the cards and asked me, "where is your husband?" Carolina answered, "He left me and went home, you said you did not see men," she replied, "Yes, but I want to see him, it in the cards it says I must see him... "

We established a nice friendship with Nalda, she was much older than us, very religious and calm. In the bathroom of the apartment, Nalda had a "biscuit" doll, very old and very beautiful, the first time Carolina entered that toilet, the doll bent forward and returned to its original position. Carolina almost got out running, scared, she told Nalda, "the doll in the bathroom bent forward when I entered and closed the door," ahh ... Nalda said, "She stoops to greet the good people", she said ... "and she recognized that you are very good, so she greeted you "... several times we asked Nalda to read the cards for us and we were very surprised at so much detail, so accurate of past events, private (no one knew, only Carolina and myself knew) and future events that were happening. Nalda was right "fortunately", when she predicted that we would "win the lottery or something," well, not exactly "winning the lottery", but you are going to receive a very large amount of money, which is due to you and she also predicted a second and a third time that we would receive unexplained amounts of money, so it was!!!!...

When traveling by car, you have to respect traffic regulations, if you have to take the longest journey to get somewhere, you'd better do that, if you take the "shortcut" and you go against the flow of traffic, you may cause accidents, have faith and follow the rules, it's the best...

Right from an early age, whilst living in England, the birthplace of the Insurance industry, and one of the main insurance places in the world, I have purchased several insurance policies for different events and for different periods. When I fi, I purchased a policy to leave some money if I died then I purchased other policies until I learned about the "life" policy, which is paid if you continue alive after specific events, illnesses or accidents. This seemed like a good idea because if one has an accident, one does not necessarily dies, one can survive and have after effects...I know about that...and I know it very well...

21
Illnesses, Cancer....

Carolina had a medical checkup and Suzana, a doctor, brunette about 45 years of age, well known for her studies and conferences, did further analysis, she discovered that a breast lump was a tumour and needed to operate it, it was an aggressive cancer, in its early stages. It happened that exactly at that time, I developed a problem with my appendix, in pain and had to be operated. Both Carolina and me were in the hospital for different reasons, we shared the same hospital room, not the same bed, but almost ... at least a very nice room, when a doctor entered the room, we would ask, which one of us do want to see...? We joked within our limitations, because of our surgeries.

During our first visit to Nalda, she told us that Carolina's surgery had been a success and she was cured, but Simon ... I worry that there is something wrong there, something has not gone well with your surgery, they will having to operate you again within one year. Nalda, I said, they removed the appendix, it was a simple operation, and there cannot be any complications. Well there are, you have to return to the doctor, she explained to me and indeed, during operation, a nerve had been damaged and it was causing extreme pain, the pain was increasing as time went on, while walking, sitting, in any position , it increased with the passing time, of the weeks and months. Several doctors examined me and thought there was nothing more that they could do, I had to endure the pain until the Doctor Erick, student of difficult cases, decided to operate again and "cure" the nerve, similar to the treatment of a nerve at the base of a tooth, he was right, the pain finally stopped and we went back to Nalda and told her that she was right!!!!! It was amazing, I had the operation in the time you had indicated and the reason that you had indicated!!!

Ahh, but what about the life insurance we bought in London?, was not for cancers?, yes, it was, including the type of cancer that Carolina had. We request payment of the insured amount, they sought not one but a thousand reasons to avoid paying, we disputed with lawyers and did not reach any agreement, the case was referred to the Ombudsman, who could not find words, literally could not find words out of his own mess, he contradicted himself, like a "beginner", complaint after complaint, just to give the reason to the insurer not to pay, but with arguments that seemed to have been written by the insurance company and not by the Ombudsman. Can you believe?

They argued that Carolina had a mis-carriage, a natural abortion and we had not declared it, at the time we took on the insurance, as if it had been a disease and then, as we omitted to declare that information, they invalidated the insurance cover, for what they should have paid, for an event (breast cancer), which had no connection with the natural abortion. What a disappointment, the system just as I had in my mind, I had always appreciated for its justice and independence, had been "pushed to one side" to decide in favour of the "vested interests", I did not think the "system" could get away from the truth, it took me a while to realize that earthly justice is theoretical and in practice it is dominated by the "created" interests, the so-called "god dollar" (currency), I realized the difference between the earthly god and the God of the Universe. My faith in the system had collapsed, my faith in men had been broken. Man finds it difficult to do the simplest thing, to do the right things, without the self-interest, without the interest of the boss interfering, without the interest in the "money" factor, we do not realize that these are the interests of the god of evil!!! Life is more beautiful, the simpler one lives it, but how easy it is complicate it, not doing what is right. Indeed, I do not learn, I'm relying on the good will of men ... it is enough if there is just one ... and there is always someone that crosses your path, having good intentions and acts in good faith. Hurray!!! !!! So Simon, you know now?

One can see a plant grow and do nothing, but you can also add fertilizer to it, prune it, water it and surely the better cared for plant, will be in better shape and also give better fruits. If you are like a plant, you deserve care, fertilizer, watering, that will make you a good plant and will give better results, don't you think ?, no matter which religion one follows, or even without following any particular religion, does it not appear just a simple and logical way to live? Is money important?, accumulate it with material things?, a plant does not fertilize or waters itself, is not one person that waters and fertilizes that plant? We are like a plant, being sufficiently attractive for someone to worry about us, watering us, pruning us, is not the same then as "behaving well" and doing the right things...do you understand Simon???

22
The Pure Energy

Having our arms near one another, it felt like an electric current, which made us get closer together, it gave us pleasure, we were attracted, we felt relaxed, but it was not in our minds to fall in love, we were just friends. We talked a lot, really a lot, nonstop, we had many experiences throughout our lives complemented each other, without realizing it, we were eager to learn more from each other, really being interested each other, more than friendship, true love came about, Carolina and I decided to get married. How come?, right in front of our common friends?, yes, our friends of our lifetime, were all witnesses to our reunion and we continued forward, was it a risk?, of course, nobody wants to risk "failure" in front of all their common friends. Instead, we decided to keep quiet, "low profile" moving away from our common friends and dedicating ourselves to our new home, our new family would have to be the focus of our future. We sought for help in books, on how to make a home in a second marriage and how to incorporate her existing children. The children became the centre of the home, without pressure from one side or another, the truth had to be shared with them first, sharing everything with them, making them participate, with respect and keeping everyone in their own position and own role, without interfering. We had many new experiences, much happiness, great pain of separation which became necessary for travel, for study, for growth. Releasing more rope to give more freedom, staying close but not "on top". We did what we thought would be best to deliver them to the University of life. University as in universal, studies, pleasures, duties, respect, trying to get the balance body/soul.

There is a saying "a word to the wise is enough", well I have to admit that I was a very bad listener and many words and many deeds were necessary for me to understand.... In the business world, I was very interested in the money to buy property, live comfortably, enjoy life and do good things and help others?, but that was not the end goal. The good times are seven and the lean times are also seven?, business was good, but it can also go wrong and it happens in reality, life has taken me through very extreme, dangerous situations, some very comfortable ... and if the ceiling in your office collapses (happily without any personal injury), and if you have a water leak at home and you find out that the bill is over US$ 20 thousand? And why you lost your brother, your best friend and your girlfriend... do you understand Simon?

Our next door neighbour was very surprised, she looked at my wife and said, frightened, Carolina, you have a light around your head!!!, how can that be? she replied, but the neighbour confirmed that she could see a light all around Carolina's head...

At the supermarket, my wife was alone in an afternoon, there were few customers, she was going around pushing the shopping trolley, when suddenly a lady who was pushing her own shopping trolley and was walking from the opposite direction, stopped and said, Madam, you have a light around your head !!...

Just as a clean mirror reflects everything very clearly, a tarnished mirror obscures a clear picture and sometimes does not allow to see anything, a tanned person looks great, another with internal peace, may look all its splendour, with its aura more visible to others. It's not just one event, there are many and very extreme and extraordinary episodes, I just record some here, hard to believe right?, well, I find it hard to believe myself, but there are so many events and many others recorded by other people....well, you know, I mean it's not an invention, these are real and true facts, which I share with you, for us to learn together. Just as a future mother has an obligation to care for herself and for her child in her womb, to give it the best chance in life, we all have an obligation to care for and feed our soul, so that when our body stops working (do you understand? ... when the body dies!), when our soul leaves our body, it can follow the path of eternity in heaven. I repeat not once but many times, I was there and also in hell, they both exist!!! and they are just like the reputations they have, heaven is infinitely better !!! We continually receive direct and indirect indications, just as the collapse of the roof of the office was a direct message to leave that place, the rocks at the mouth of the river.... We had been near to my mother in the last few years of her life, "visiting" at her home and one night I was just sitting on my bed, getting ready to sleep when I heard a noise of metal and glass "crash" !!, Carolina coming behind me shouted "aaayyy !!!!" someone broke the front door of the house !! ???, no..., we saw glass near the kitchen door, as we got closer, we saw that a wall cupboard was on the floor, the cupboard had been fixed to a wall for years, yet it had fallen off, over the the table and then against the sink and the floor, breaking dishes and whatever else was inside, but Carolina had been drinking a glass of water there, just seconds before the accident ... !!!, it was clear, we had to make plans to move, plan to live somewhere else. Simon, once again, do you understand?

23
More Signals

I was with my wife the other day in a small town, we parked the car and in a careless moment, wile getting off the car, my wife banged her head on the edge of the car door, she hit it very hard in the forehead, close to her right eye, I went close to her, are you well? Does it hurt much? and I said, I have to get some ice for that not to get worse!!!, I turned around and I saw a truck coming down the street towards us, stopping next to me, the truck had written very large signs in the front and on the sides, hey read: "ICE", the driver descended from the truck, he approached me and asked me: do you want ICE?, we laughed, despite the pain Carolina had... it was an ice delivery truck, sure, a very normal event, what was so funny, was that normally, the driver of those trucks, do no stop and offers ice to the first person in his way, this was just when we wished to get some ice ... we requested. coincidence?, signal?

When we moved in to live together in London with Carolina, the first time we received the electricity bill, the bill showed a credit value!!! The electricity bill came quarterly and unbelievably, in the first quarter we lived together with Carolina, the bill came in credit, so there was nothing to pay, on the contrary, we had "generated" energy and the we had "sold" that back to the electricity distribution company ... an example of what man can do... very powerful !!!!! ...that was also a true fact, never before and never after have had we had such a situation...!!! Pity, all other accounts show values that we have to pay...!!! hahaha...

Our appointment with Dr. Mary ended after the consultation, she asked us to wait a few minutes in the waiting and then she returned very happy, smiling to say that the result was positive!!! we were going to be parents !!! Carolina should go to see a specialist, where we went as quickly as we could, Dr. Peter assured us that everything was normal and after a few weeks we saw on the screen was a little girl, who was developing normally ... that gave us so much joy. !!! There could not be anything above this, we dreamt, we had plans, we shared the happiness with our closest!!!... A few months later, on the night of 31st August 1997, Carolina began to feel ill and there was blood, we hurried to the hospital, there were no emergency patients, we arrived at the time news were coming out that princess Diana of Great Britain had died in a car crash in Paris, the nurse confirmed to us the news that Carolina was having a miscarriage, a spontaneous abortion, more tears, all our hopes vanished in an instant. Simon, do you understand?, these are signs, signals, don't you understand?

Carolina, why not you answer the phone?, I asked my wife and she said: answer the phone? but it is not ringing... and instantly the phone started ringing, she answered and had a long and pleasant conversation with her sister ... and so , several times, it strikes us as sometimes, I feel the first sign of the phone and then the phone rings ... really we should try with the phone on "silent" mode... hahaha !!!

I was there having lunch with another Brazilian friend and engaged in interesting conversation, but at any moment, I asked her: "Why are you crying?" he said, but I'm not crying, then mobile phone rang, it was her mother, she asked to be excused, she talked for about two or three minutes and ended the conversation, crying ... how did you know I'd cry?, she asked me... an example of messages or signals that I receive, but am unable to clarify details, my communication is still incipient, complex and incomplete, I am still looking for ways to improve or understand them and I keep asking for help from the good souls to guide me in these matters. I have full confidence that there is something more behind all this, hopefully I will have time to understand...

My wife has several brothers and sisters, Carolina had a special bond with her father, Georg, she was the most expressive of all his daughters and sons. Her father was a person who had read and studied a lot, including theology and philosophy. When her father was over 80, he was with poor health, he was in pain from his cancer he had, he went through chemotherapy, but it was not getting better. Daddy, when you die, send me a sign to tell me if there is something beyond..., lol... yeah right, I'll phone you said Georg and he laughed...

We kept on visiting him over time and between trips, we went to visit her father, in fact, to say goodbye to him, he was in a coma and we had a long trip to Europe that night, via North America. The nurse told us that he did not hear, he was not responding, but approaching him, he opened his eyes and Carolina was able to tell him how much she loved him, as all his children also did and how proud she was of him, not to be afraid and told him that God was waiting for him. We said goodbye to to him, indicating "see you later." Just when we reached the midpoint of travel, in North America, we learned that had already left, but went ahead with our journey, because we were ready and we had very important commitments in Europe, that Georg would have not liked that we cancelled.

Upon arriving home in London, it was very late and we went directly to sleep, but after midnight, the phone rang, I answered hello ... hello ... hello ... but there was no answer and then I checked with the automatic service detecting the origin of the call received, I heard a message that said "you have received a call from an unknown number." I went back to bed, Carolina asked me, who called? your dad I said, what!!?? who?? !!... If it was my dad, he should pone again!!!

The following night, I woke up to the phone ringing, at the same time after midnight hello ... hello ... hello ... and no answer, but the detection system, informing the origin of the last call said "you have received a call from an unknown number " the message informed me. So I went back to bed, Carolina asked me who called? And told her what had happened and she told me, then yes... it was my dad!!!, he must have arrived at the "other place".

Some years passed and my wife saw in a magazine of an airplane, an article on several studies of "after death communication" (ADC's), made in the USA and Great Britain, where it was reported by the studies that there are many cases of people who say they have received phone calls from their loved ones, after they have deceased.

Back in South America, we attended a family reunion, Carolina's family, where several relatives who lived in different countries were visiting for the gathering. We told them of our experience of the phone calls we had received and some thought that may have been possible, others thought that could not have happened. When we got ready to leave for a restaurant for dinner, the phone in the house rang, someone went to answer and said hello ... hello ... hello ... and no one on the line. Dad, ... no, ... cannot be ... the phone rang for a second time, hello ... hello ... hello ... and no one was on the line. My dad...!!! Silence ... well, if he called again ... and surely, the phone rang again .hello...hello

... hello...and there was nobody on the line. In silence, we left, everyone thinking that Georg might actually had phoned as he had said that he would do.

Is there such thing as Marriage by "medical recommendation"?, I am convinced that there is, due to the experience Carolina had, when she was diagnosed a tumour in the ovary at age 20 and by the magnitude of the size of the tumour, the surgeon had to remove an ovary, it was cancerous, the specialists predicted that she would soon lose the other ovary, so they recommended that she continued a fertility treatment, to quickly have a family. This is documented in the medical records of those dates and with much happiness and success, Carolina had two gorgeous children who enjoy perfect health, sympathy and success.

After 20 years, we had the opportunity to talk with the doctors who treated Carolina for ovarian cancer and his reaction was "Carolina? You're alive?", because they never thought she would survive for long, nor that she would be a person so full of life, joy and love. The documentation confirms that the will of our "Big Boss" is what counts, Carolina and I shared so many experiences and each one is becoming more extreme, that amazes us, we are very happy and that is the reason why we want to share everything with you, not with all, with you in particular. Cancer is a disease that disturbs many people, it can actually be lived through and controlled, with love, understanding, sharing and asking for help from others, not only around us, we know that there are souls, mostly from our past relatives that are there, around us, to which we can turn to, to ask for help and help them. Not all had the joy of being with the ticket to eternity with them at the time of their deaths, but we really have the opportunity to help their reconciliation and why should they not help us too, if we ask for it?, is it that we are so selfish?, is that we don't have faith?, it is worth checking that out ... for sure it will not hurt you...

Both, at the time of the ovarian cancer, and also at the breast cancer's that threatened Carolina, there were very worthy moments that deserve mention, especially in Porto Alegre, Brazil, where the treatment of Radiotherapy was performed, at the centre where treatment was applied, a place, where all kinds of people were together, some very poor, some appeared to be very wealthy, men, women, young and old, the reason for all to be there, was one, receiving radiotherapy to destroy the remnants of various cancers that affected each of those people, without distinction.

That waiting room, was one of the most "holy" places that we have found anywhere, there was so much fervour, all praying, each one concentrated in their own case or that of the people they accompanied, that energy, that divine will, is not lost, it gets multiplied and we have to recognize, I have no doubt that even the walls of that room, were full of positive energy, positive thoughts, no envy, no materialism, or idolatry, it is possible to get those things, just trying a little and you can, but beware, there we are always those looking for to attract us with temptation leading us into alienation, forgetfulness, and the temporary earthly convenience, have faith, it is worth continuing. Do you understand Simon? Ahhh... even worse, do you feel like being the idol? You have been made the idol of others?, be careful with your pride, simplicity, you're not the only one, nor are you "inventing" anything new, do you remember John Paul II?, people loved him, was he idolized?, he never felt "superior" (at least he did not show it), he never lost his simplicity, humility, and that made the people love him more ... do you understand Simon?

24
The Continuity Of Life...The Ticket To Eternity...

Ahhh and is this why you ended up in the hospital with pain in the appendix and whom you love so much, also ended up in hospital with cancer ?, these are perfectly valid questions and they have answers too, that's the reason why you married someone you love so much, so you will have the opportunity to love others and tell them what you have learned, share your knowledge, worry about others, the ticket you need cannot be bought with money, but with love, love for the others, that's why you were shown paradise and hell, for you to decide your eternal destiny and to help others decide theirs. Faith in God, faith that he will guide you, care for you, faith in the child you were, that was the foetus that was in your mother's womb, no one remembers the moment they left their mother's womb, we only know about it because someone told us about it, that is faith and faith in the destiny of your soul depends on you, will you do something for your soul?

The smell of a person can distinguish different scents, flowers, food, inclusive of people, but each of us has the smell developed to varying degrees, and everyone has different tastes and preferences of odours that may be preferred or be disliked. What I like does not have to be what you like or the others like, nor the smell I consider to be pleasant, must be nice to others. You cannot ask me to like the smell of cinnamon, if that is the favorite smell of one of my loved ones or idols. We have to know how to identify yourself and have your own identify and not wanting to just assimilate "fashions" of the others. No two runners reach always together the first place, that may be a "draw", it is very difficult to have two, but to have three, together all the time, is almost impossible.

One must make do with what one has, we may want more, but if it does not arrive, as we've heard before, "it must be for a reason". Everyone has their own qualities, gifts, skills, passions, and how we all get to the same end? We all live in homes, in cities, towns or isolated places, all walk, drink water and take food, we breathe, the have food, we digest, then how we will not have the same end ?, seeing conversely, we are all born of a mother and we will all arrive at same end as. Ahh... but on the way we can follow any of the routes, professions or activities that we saw, some successful, some not so much, some full of problems, some happy and others envious, spiteful or greedy... ahhh... that is a difference, in the end we all know that in our passage through this life on earth, we are all "born" when we become autonomous and leave the womb of our mothers, and our soul will cease to exist in our body and " will be born" into eternal life or "in the afterlife" when our bodies stop functioning and we die.

Or don't you remember how it was when you were inside your mother's womb? Don't you believe?, you don't think you were born from your mother's womb?, yes, you were and that is Faith, believing what one is told. Who was your grandmother?, you need more FAITH to believe that the person they tell you was your grandmother, she really was. Well, it's the same in your mother's womb you were an egg coupled with a sperm and that combination grew, it was fed by your mother, but you will say, that there you did not have skills, you did not cry or breathed, nor felt flavours...?, are you sure?, do you remember? ...At the end of the day you go to bed and fall asleep, well, at the end of life is the same as it was at the beginning, you continue with another form of existence, just as when you left your mother's womb, you start to breathe. With the death of your body on earth, your soul starts the eternal life, it is your birth into eternity. The soul is what you have had had since you left your mother's womb and you have nourished and developed throughout your life. There are souls that grow to be good and there are souls that end up with evil, it's your choice, bahh... it was the same when your mother had the choice of joining with your father, they both selected each other and then you were born; the new creature that you are preparing, you yourself can form it, so that your soul would be, just as you would like it to be and you will release it into eternity with the death of your body.

You will tell me, and if I do not feed my soul, if I don't work on developing it ?, that doesn't interest me, I do not believe in that stuff .. !!! Well, there are girls who say they prefer to have fun when they meet with a guy, but you see? When there is a baby to be born, there will be a birth, there is no "half birth". Putting water freeze, will turn to ice, dying undoubtedly will release your soul into the eternity, it is a fact that it will take place and you have no options.

How do I feed my soul? Let's say that you want to be a nurse, then you take some courses, you study, you practice, you learn. If you want to feed your soul, you study, you practice, you ask for help to those that know how to make souls grow, it's not about giving your soul away and to say would you please form my soul!!!, it is you yourself that has to do that.

When you are born from your mother's womb, you have no choice, you leave her body and you have to start breathing and when you are born into eternal life it is the same, your soul leaves your body and you have start "breathing" the eternal light.

Studies indicate that within the womb, the foetus can recognize sounds, voices, music and even smells. You can see the foetus reacting, and even smiling to certain stimuli, the child after birth can "recognize" them as known, sure, we can in this life recognize experiences that occurred "before birth" do you understand ?, then there nothing odd about talking of some experiences of our soul after death and the start of eternal life.

Do you remember when you were in your mother's womb?, the music she listened?, the love she gave you? No ?, and if someone were to be remembered once having been partying before birth ?, if someone explained how "life" was inside the womb, would you believe it ?, so, why would you not believe what some people have already experienced, what have happened to them in the state of "soul" after death! Taboo?

A doctor studies medicine has to follow training, does exams and finally has his or hers medical degree and title. Does that mean that they will never read a book of medicine again?, will they be a good doctor "always" only by studying his medical course ?, most likely they continually have to read, study, attend courses, lectures and give talks, always progressing, updating themselves. A woman, knowing that she will be a mother does everything possible for her child to be born with the right weight and she takes care in her food, activities and is careful about anything or anyone that might disturb her child? We also know what it is good and what is bad in life, but are we concerned constantly developing this knowledge? or let what is more "tempting" (evil), take control of our lives ?, is it not easier for the doctor to simply devote his time to watching sports on TV, instead of reading another book of medicine?

A doctor may also smoke, drink alcohol, he knows that excesses are harmful to health, but that it does not make him a "better" or a "worse" doctor, it could be argued that even that he can learn from these situations, he can say that he could understand better their patients. We all have behaviours or moments in our lives that are not pleasant and can be as reprehensible, but if we recognize, learn and move on without being "dragged" by the current, we can make sure that we take care of our "baby soul" to be, that we carry with us, so that we can make sure of their entry into the eternal paradise and not into the eternal suffering. Is it not important to have the right ticket to eternity?

Have you ever seen a tree ?, it was born from a seed, but before that it was a flower on another tree (it was the mother tree) and when the tree falls down of old age (or is cut), it becomes firewood or compost or paper or ashes... and follows the cycle into eternity.

We decided to have family soon, considering the age, it was best to have quickly a family. The Chief will know how to guide us and do what is best for us. My wife, Caroline, had a very beautiful pregnancy, we lived it with joy and enthusiasm, there was a sudden loss which made us very sad and made us think a lot. That life surely would have been too far for us, and surely would not have been able to dedicate sufficiently and the Boss decided to lead it away from us.

We were required to do other things!! Simon, are you learning...?

The genes we receive from our parents at conception, give us the characteristics that we have as human beings. Generally parents that have Asian origins, have children with Asian features, parents with diabetes, leaving great possibility that your children are diabetics, alcoholics or obese and other characteristics are inherited, say embedded or become part of the information that is recorded in our genome ("chip") and then govern our lives. It is then reasonable to think that your soul, that will live the eternal life, would have the characteristics that you give it during the course of your life?, is not reasonable to think you can "train" your soul for eternal life?, remember what I was saying about the saints, who are rewarded for their eternal life and continue to help others in their transitory life?

How a child is born and how a soul is born?

Human beings have a life from the moment of birth from his mother's womb until they die. Even before birth from the womb of the mother, the child was a foetus, it had a life of 9 months. The truth is that embryo, the foetus was formed by two parts that existed long before, an egg, which had been formed for years and a sperm, both were prepared to form the foetus, prepared with love and sexual desire, much experience, all these and other elements were used to "load" the information into the "chips" that eventually became operational at the time the child left his mother's womb.

Could you tell me if a movie begins at the start of its projection? Or when the shooting starts? Or maybe when the actors and actresses who will participate in the film are born? And when does the film ends? when its projection ends?, Or when the last comment of the observers ends? Or when you "delete" it from the mind of every one of the spectators ?, the truth is that the film continues recorded and may be viewed, reviewed and even edited many times and the participants will remain "live" whenever you see them . The truth is that everything is part of a chain of events that seems to have no real start and much less a "final". They are part of the "continuity" (eternal) life.

The soul receives all the negative and positive "charges" during our lives, this decides at the moment the soul enters into eternal life, whether it goes into heaven or hell (well, those places that we decided to call them like that, but I think you understood Simon ...?). During life we fill with qualities, virtues or characteristics our soul, it would be the same as programming the "chips" of the soul, or the DNA information of the soul, if you want to see from another point of view, we are adding "brownie points", or if you want to interpret it in yet another way, we let our soul accumulate data in the "hard disk", we are "buying" the ticket to eternal ticket life and "paying" for gradually, in parts, of course not using commercial money from our day to day use, but using the supernatural "money", these are the virtues, feelings, honesty, truth, love, happiness, forgiveness, they are all very useful "coins"...!!

Do you remember Simon?, each ant, however small, does a job, it works in collaboration with others, it will not be judged by the trees that it failed to move, but the granules it had to move and ant that lived in the desert, had different objectives to the one that lived in the tropics ... do you understand Simon?, and if an elephant stepped on the ant...?? The ant was under no fault...??? ... hahaha ... then you do not need to worry, your mission here is just where you are and around you, it is not necessary to seek to do what you have not been asked to do... I bahhh...all within reason, if you're a doctor, you will have many patients and if you are a truck driver driving, you will drive a lot in your truck and not in your partner's truck, each one within their scope and surroundings ... Simon ... understood?

So that you could be born, your mother had a sexual relationship with your father, having sex is prohibited?, ugly? taboo? ... look how many people are around you, we are all born of a mother and all of them have had sex with a man to beget us, this is a "forbidden" topic or as natural as that has always existed ? One should not have shame, or be ashamed of these issues, nor about the formation of our souls, it is the most natural event, that has always existed...!!!

My young neighbour Lilly, was the daughter of a very religious family, they were proud that Lilly worked in London, had a good job and lived well, had many friends and travelled a lot. Lilly began to gain weight, but it was ... because she was expecting family, relatives worried, "horror"!!!, but you are not married ... that's not right, it is not "acceptable" ... everything continued its course until Shawn was born, her son, all was forgotten, as the greatest joy was having a new family member, the birth was an event full of happiness ... do you understand Simon ...??

Everything earthly, is accommodated in the course of our lives, but do not forget the "before" birth and what comes "after" our carnal death ... I insist, please do not forget to prepare your soul !!! Do not forget the great power of evil and that the god of evil (devil) exists, he is the ruler of that very hot ugly place you visited, Simon, do not stop asking the Grand Chief of the Good (God), to help you in the fight against evil and help all who want their souls to come to this beautiful place. There are those who can fight, some may win in the fight against evil, but if you do not win ... you lose everything, it is your soul and eternal life ...just a little humility, be humble and ask for help, that will do a lot of good for you. Do you understand Simon?

25
Parapraxes

Walking, walking, walking, travelling, travelling, travelling, do you like it?, does it satisfy you?, makes you proud?, do you get tired and very tired?, it means constantly changing environments, schedules, meals, people, scenes, temperatures, climates and even language...

Today is Monday, this is London, it seems that I had slept very little, I was wanting to do many things that day, I started very early in the morning, on the bus, then the train, almost running, had a lot to do, meetings, appointments and even dinner, got the time for everything ... and back on the train to the hotel... hooey!!!

The train compartment was packed ... it was hot and I was tired ...I had never before fallen asleep standing up, that was the first time ... I do not recommend it, when I began to fall asleep, I began to slip to the floor, towards my right side , ... yes, to the floor ... where else could it be .... ??? Really embarrassing, falling to the floor in front of all those people...hahaha...
Tuesday it was Madrid, and on Wednesday, Genoa, Vienna on Thursday and Friday ... Paris ... phew!!! Another tiring journey, next stop, another plane, another

flight, and good now it is the weekend ... how tired!! ... I slept a lot and woke up in a very large bed, I got up and went to look out the window, it was a tall building, I must have been about fifteen floors up in the hotel ... yes, it was a room in a hotel ... but where was that hotel...? I was about to panic !!!, I had lost track of where I was ... definitely I knew I was in a hotel, sure enough, a hotel, there was a telephone in the room, but what should I do ?, call the hotel reception to ask where I was ???, that would automatically qualify me as being "mad", better still, "crazy" or "looney" ... really. !!!,

I would not only appear to be crazy, I was really crazy !!!, and was getting desperate, wanting to know where was place it was totally unknown to me, well, at least I knew I was safely in a hotel ... but what city???, which Country...??? I could not find anything written about the city, the hotel had a common name, like any hotel, in English, "Grand Hotel", but that did not mean much, it could be anywhere in the world, do you know what it is to be "totally lost" without "being lost" and die of shame to ask anyone where I was... ???, I came to my senses, I sat at the foot of the bed and began to review the days of the week ... Monday was London, Tuesday Madrid, Wednesday Genoa, Thursday Vienna, Friday Paris ...I looked out the window again, that had not even the slightest hint of being Paris ... then I remembered the itinerary, after Paris, I would go to Brazil, but I had never been to Brazil ... I looked again very carefully out of the window of the building, so that I would not be scared... !!! ... yes, this should be Brazil, despite the fact that I could only see buildings, streets, cars, some people down there walking ... I tried, I tried a long time and with a lot of will to convince myself that it was Brazil ...I was scared, I phoned the front desk and asked if I could have breakfast ... judging by how the receptionist responded and I felt much more relaxed, she had a "rhythm" when she spoke, that sounded tropical, it had to be Brazil!!!... and that's how I discovered this Country ... I'm sure there are easier ways to get to know Brazil ... but this is the way I got to know that Country...hahaha... ... ...

There was one night when I had to make another long journey, it was a plane flight, but I was so tired, without any strength at all and I was sound asleep, on that trip was when I felt a strong movement of my bed, not really wanting to wake up, I thought probably it was a violent earthquake, "it will soon finish", I had no strength, nor the will to get up and have to leave for protection, the movement continued, very severe and lengthy, the movement was getting very violent and lasting a long time, it must be a massive earthquake, so finally, I decided it was time to get up and go to find a safer place now !!! It was at that point that I tried to get up, but I could not because I was lying, but with a belt that did not allow me to get up, was across several seats on an airplane, with blankets, pillows and tried to get up during the supposed "earthquake" I was experiencing, I woke up and felt greatly embarrassed!!!, it was a serious error, oops!!!, shame...!!! It was not an earthquake, it was a simple, but very severe turbulence that we were flying through uuuhhh!!!, luckily no one saw my incoherence ... uuuuhhh !!! A slip ... involuntary... they say it happens even in the best of families ...hahaha !!!

When entering a lift, you do not control the movement of the vehicle, it is as if you would be in a car, in a train or a plane and you cannot really do anything to control it. That fact is that you require faith, faith is the confidence one has on the vehicle in which one is traveling, faith in the people that made it, in those that programmed it for the successful operation of the "vehicle" to move, to go from one place to another place, in bad weather, in a hurry, just for a ride, alone or in company, in any situation.

We heard noise, there is a very strong turbulence?, storm? I asked the passenger sitting next to me ?, I do not know, said my friend Charlie who was two seats away, bad weather out there ?, ahhh... then I have to sleep a little longer, I answered, I have no control over this situation. The problem is not mine, there is a commander in the plane and that's his problem,
I want to sleep ... That's what faith is about, it is so simple Simon, do you agree?

Sleeping ?, someone said "sleeping" ?, It is very easy, but so easy to do and it may also be "unusual" in certain situations like when I slept floating in a swimming pool, another time whilst floating in the sea and even in the dentist's chair, while he was working on my teeth !!! ahh... not forgetting the day I made the journey to heaven and hell, I felt just as if I had fallen asleep, meaning that it was going from a state of being "awake" to the state of being "asleep" and from the state of being "alive" to the state of being "dead" they are simply different "states" of existence.

26
The Roasted Meat

If you know how to cook, you know that meat can be grilled or fried, if you do it a very short time then the result is a juicy, tasty, tender meat... but according to your taste and way of cooking, meat can also be cooked for longer or can be fried in little or too much oil, as the case may be... which form is tastier and better in the end ?, clearly that depends on your preference or that of those who will consume the meat... and what about the meat that was fried in oil, maybe in too much oil and maybe in oil that had previously been used... what are the effects... ??? if you chose the frying route, it is best to "clean" or remove of excess fat and above all it is better to better quality... you know what happens if you continually use "bad" or too much oil?, sure, there may be several problems, cleaning the kitchen, there may be health and even environmental problems... you should not do the same with your life, you should stop accumulating "dirt", or impure elements which just build up and cause the "disasters" of which we then complain and report... it is so much easier and pleasant to have fun, make others smile, share and give happiness to others. Difficult?, you saw there are trees that produce very hard wood and others produce with very soft wood and are prone to termites and attacks by other wood insects... you do not choose the "wood" that one is made of, our internal tree, but we do have the option of caring for our internal "wood", we should give it maintenance to avoid damage and that we do not harm others ... Simon ... do you understand?

Remember that we talked about the rocks, the stones, the "perfect" beings of this universe, which are already fully developed and need no further "development" because they are "perfect", well, we're not those, we are still learning and developing ourselves... surely you remember seeing the sun "rise" one day and seeing it "setting" or hiding ...have you thought?, the following day the sun "rises again" and has another "setting", it is like being "born" and "dying" in the same day...or is it like us, when we are born, we come from "before" and we continue in an "after", but we are always changing. The sun is not the same from one day to the next, it has different "positions" from one day to the next, it has explosions, movement, it gets closer to our earth or it can be further away. It makes us warmer in the summer and at the same time keeps some of us cooler in winter, don't tell me that the sun is bipolar ...hahaha...the sun is much nicer than some of us...hahaha...

The sun enlightens, warms us up, helps us with our crops... our ancestors worshiped the sun as their god, we can also worship the sun, especially when we're on holidays, but we do not consider today the sun as our god, however we adore chocolates, mobile phones, cars, they make us feel that we have power, are you sure you are not considering them as gods?? ... Be attentive Simon!!!

27
The Ceiling Collapsed In The London Office

Go on and on, led by the "wave" of the sea, because the pace of life drags you, just because "you cannot go back", because you are already committed to the way of life around you... ahhh... what will other people say??? !!! ...the critics, the denials, accusations, hatreds, desires, the envy ... other people ... but you maintain your "goals" clear, firm, fixed, as per your own desires and objectives ?, One "harvests" from others too, their "waves", both negative and positive ...you require a clear and definite effort to attract only those positive waves, to help you achieve your goals ... be careful, evil is very quick and clever and is always looking for ways to block your work ...do you understand Simon ??

The company where you worked, had people that were ideal for the job they were performing, it was a select, very professional, creative, friendly, pleasant, positive team and worked in a comfortable, almost familiar atmosphere, plans were drawn and entirely achievable goals set ... achievements succeeded regularly, there was a balance between getting financial returns, acquire knowledge, develop friendships, helping others, all within the cosy setting ...yes eventually appeared the "characters" sent by the "envy team", to cause trouble, "wallowing" and cast doubts, with the sole purpose to create destruction of business, relationships and that pleasant environment. There had already been several experiences with attacks against the business people trying to "tear down" the activity, but they persisted, persevered, taking advantage of certain times where you were "distracted", distant and perhaps in weak health, making it easier to fall into temptation and selfishness, for them "to do their thing"... driving business away, obstructing, who would have imagined,... they were getting their way, slowly, a bit at a time, first quietly, then directly, even blatantly... would you believe that at night, without any warning ... the ceiling in the office "collapsed", it caved in ... for no apparent reason, without any physical event to explain it, yeah ... the ceiling "collapsed", fortunately without any personal injury, but how was it ... why ?? Who did it???, there are those who speak and know of energies that would surely be much more qualified than I am to try to explain ... what I would say is true ... Simon, Simon ??!! Do you understand?, what did you do to prevent evil from penetrating your environment? Being attacked by evil?

What happens when an eclipse of the sun takes place? Or simply when there is a sunset?, Is the sun not to back out the next day? or at the end of the eclipse? Is it that the sun "died"? does it have a different temperature?... there might be some variations undoubtedly, very well Simon, the same with your life, continue with the journey, through the barriers and the joys...

We wanted more space for our home, we decided it was time to make changes, leave the green residential area of London (read "expensive" area ...), where spaces for living, to get around, to travel, not only every day were narrower, but also became crowded areas, we could say that the area was already "too much in demand" many people, wanted to live in London, the demand seemed "unreal".

Having lived over 30 years in the same area of London had left many experiences and there was nostalgia, emotions, a lifetime, where initially there was a cute, clean, friendly neighbourhood, really a village within London and then to see it filled with so many people, attracted by all the material things around. There were burglaries, assaults, in all the apartments around us, in most of the cars parked around, in the gardens of those big houses, surrounded by large, old trees, full of tradition, a woman was raped and "no one noticed" no one saw, or heard anything, "impersonality" had arrived. Nobody was interested in anyone that was more than 5cm away from anyone's nose... it was not natural, all deep down are brothers, cousins, relatives, we are a family and we failed to recognize it, we all wanted to be different, being separate, selfish, independent, without realizing that we depend on each other for our successes and our daily life.

Who can say that Moses was not a relative of theirs?, far enough in the past... surely even Adam himself has certainly been a relative of mine too ... and yours !!!, that's really cool !!! ... why nobody told me that before?? ... hahaha ... surely even the ants understand that one of them alone, doesn't get to do much... all that is done in "community" gets them to achieve wonders!!!...do you understand Simon?? It is true, one is really concerned with those that are around you, in their immediate surroundings, "you're okay" one says to another, of course, wish him well, "I forgive you", we know it's good to forgive, but why only in your immediate surroundings?, could you not wish well to your ancestors? And help them to ask for forgiveness too?, If you talk with your God, don't you think it would be good for you to ask him to forgive your ancestors? ... Think about it ... Simon!!!

We changed the small apartment occupying part of an old house, built over a century ago, with walls so thick that seemed almost like a "castle" (well, say "a little castle ..."), but with so many problems of cracks, air leaks, rain filtering, and really did not justify the trouble ..we were attracted by a new house, "zero kilometres" which would just be completed to build, ahhhh... we will no longer have to be fixing anything ... everything is in good working order... well... yummy !!!

There were differences, of course, we would have more space, stairs up and stairs to go down, a garden to take care of, a garage to fill up with "old" and "useless" stuff... hahaha... All very nice, clean, new carpets ... now we have to look after them, ... all shoes are removed upon entering the house and walk indoors only with sandals. Ahhh what a difference... that's progress for all of us, home was taking a better shape...

Who would have thought? one day we received the initial water bill, with a figure above US$ 10000 !!!! Consumption!!!??? what ... ??? Are they crazy???

We might be supplying water to the entire neighbourhood!!!, how ?, let us see, let us do some tests, we close all the taps in the house and the water meter must stop ... what ??? ... The meter is still spinning like crazy??? Surely we are supplying water to all the neighbours ... but, what if we are not...?, the house is new, we should not have more headaches !!!... but the meter was still spinning "max speed"... then we may have a water leak under the house....?, water might be eroding the foundations of the house, all the land which supports the construction and then it might even collapse... !!!, ouch!!! ... Let us call the construction company, they should have a clearer notion of what might be happening...

Being a new home, the inlet water from the mains supply from the street, was installed under the floor of the house, but inside another pipe that protected it and allowed "easily" to be "changed", without breaking the floor, walls or causing any major problems... actually, that pipe had been damaged by a nail, before it was installed in the house and had always leaked... easy, it was changed... ahh, but the water consumption... You will have to pay... we?, why? It was your failure in the first place, you failed to check the work you were doing. Not so easy, everything required arguments, evidence, photos... incredible, once again the power of the strongest is demonstrated, not the power of the truth.

The pipe was changed, we did not pay anything, well, not paid any money, but our loss was certainly in all the time we lost, effort, inconvenience, stress. Do you understand Simon??

You do not choose what obstacles you have in your life, they simply appear on your way, the elephant that appeared in front of the ant ... stepped on it... hahaha... it stopped being an ant and became food for some other insect in the world ...what a story!!! the story about the new house that was not going to give any headaches, was really awesome...do you remember Simon ??, your happiness is so different to idolatry ... human "needs" created for you and the "love" of your God which must always be above the human "love" to your loved ones...!!!

You do not choose the obstacles of life, they 'Appear, one elephant who Appeared in front of the ant... stepped on... hahaha... it stopped being an ant and then became food for some other insect in the world. is still there ... but so beautiful ...?? that was so cute, the subject of the new house without problems... remember Simon ??, your happiness is to differentiate what is idolatry and human "needs", created for you and the "love" for your God, this must always be above any the human "love" even to your loved ones ...!!!

How easy it is to have a dollar as a god, idolatry to the dollar, the mobile phone idol (god), the car idol (god), the idolatry or chocolate god and even when you convert your most beloved person on earth as an idol... do you understand Simon ??

28
Healing

We came across "Healing" again, Carolina had suffered a syncope, this was due to extreme stress we were going through, my mother had become seriously ill, due to a heart condition and I was "running around", I was approached by a nun and she told me to go to Mary, a woman who I would help me, she was a "healer". With a few directions and indications, not very clear or correct by the way, I went looking for Mary and "accidentally" ran into her in the street, ahhh, it's true, there are people that help "heal" people and there are groups of "healing", oops! , she explained, helped me, she "identified" issues in me, hummm... the truth is that I want to learn more, I want to know more about "healing"... well, it really is such a deep and broad topic, I'll leave it for another time in our "conversations".

Simon... Simon... ... ...Simon!!! wakes!!! Looks like you have not learned!!! ??? Ouch !!! How strong is that pain in my left leg !!! uh-oh!!! It is very painful below the knee, on my left calf ...but I have to work, I have an important business appointment, I must not be late... I know, I will stop at a pharmacy on the way, ouch!!, I'm in pain, and already delayed bahhh... I am sorry, will have to leave the car illegally parked for a moment.

Already in the pharmacy, I ok accept any recommendation to reduce the pain on my leg, yes please, a little water ... I kept going, I apologized for being late for my meeting, but I could only say that I was behind schedule, not that I felt any pain... shame to say that, to say that I was not feeling well would have been a sign of weakness...!!! Long busy day, at night attended a business dinner, ate at a nice restaurant, good service, very fine, plenty of drinks and finally back to sleep in the hotel, have some rest... ahhh !!! I really needed that.

Simon... Simon... wake up!!!... you never learn... Simon!!! OUCH!!! That pain on my leg is getting worse, I'd better travel early, back to the nearest town, it is just 200 kilometres away, but with each kilometre of travel, makes the pain ever more tormenting. It is just at the back of my left leg, behind the knee, the entire calf and now also my left foot... uuuhhh!!! It is getting worse... another tablet that I bought at the pharmacy... ahhh it relieves the pain slightly...I am almost there, just another half an hour driving ... if only the car was automatic, it would be less painful, I would not have to use my left leg to make the gear changes ... I remember I have seen a big hospital in the city centre, in the slope of a hill, ... yes, I see it there!!!, where would the entrance be??? I am getting very anxious... yes, it's an emergency, I can hardly walk, please could I see a doctor?, well fortunately a Dr. Hans greeted me, he heard the symptoms, he checked me, but he had some doubts as to what was the cause of the pain, it could be a blood clot in the leg, but it could also be a problem in the spine. He requested some exams and in the meantime to inject this product around the navel, that is prevent your blood from clotting, if that was the problem Dr Hans explained.

OK first the injection and then where do I get these tests done?, this city is so complicated, traffic on the street is very slow and disorganized, ouch!! pain in my left leg still increasing... I cannot drive anymore...!!! Taxi, there and taxi back, walk up the hill again ... there are people waiting for tests, but you are a foreigner, you need some additional documents, today you cannot be seen... why ?, I can hardly walk because of the pain... I'm sorry, that's the system... I am very tired, exhausted, I think I should now go to the hotel, sleep, and continue early the next day, keep searching where to get the tests done.

Wake up!!! Simon, Simon!!! aaaaaaahhhh!!!! That pain, I cannot even turn around to one side in bed, too much pain aaaahhhh !!!, ouch!!!! I cannot get out of bed... that pain is killing me!!! Now, what do I do?? Nothing changes, carry on, take a deep breath and have a shower...not possible!! I cannot bend... the pain is too strong ...ohh!!! I just got managed to put on my underwear... uuuuhhh! And the trousers, but I could not bend enough to put on my socks, it does not matter, shoes with my feet only half way into them, I am desperate and alone!!!

I am leaving the hotel now, please keep my bags, I'm going to a hospital and I do not know when I would be back for them. Taxi !!!, please take me to a hospital...

Sir, do you need information about a stay in the hospital?, but you need to come with a family member to be admitted into the hospital...you cannot be admitted if you are alone... !!! What??? Can't you see, I'm a foreigner!!!, I have no family here !!! ...let me see... well, after hours of desperate arguments, I got admission to conduct the test, in the meantime, something for the pain... oh yes, here in the emergency section we give you something for the pain, directly into the vein, this is called "Formula One", ok, shhhuure... but... nuuursee... n u u u r s e ... n u u r... the patient in the place next to me heard my fading voice... NURSE !!!! he screamed, the nurse ran back, while I was fainting, she acted immediately, raised my leg, I had badly reacted to the injection of the Formula One. Highly effective, the nurse revived me and disconnecting from my arm the flow of Formula One.

Well, you have a herniated disc in the lower spine, with rest and anti-inflammatory and analgesics you should improve, ok, let us do that, well we should keep you for about 15 days, I accepted and was admitted to the hospital!!! I had a lot of pain and was very nervous.

Would the fact that I would have to stay a few days in the hospital be offset if I had a blonde blue eyed nurse and that she had to bathe me...???... Dreams?? or desires?? ...Simon ...Simon...

Carolina travelled from afar to be with me throughout the process, tears, emotions, walking was painful and had to wait, patience, both of us were very anxious, until the day I was due to be discharged from the hospital... but it was impossible!!! ...how could it be... the pain on my leg had worsened in the last 24 hours and my right leg, which had not bothered before it was now also hurting... what could be the reason?, do one last blood test, just for safety... what ??? The result showed I had some blood clot and I could not leave the hospital, the hospital discharge was cancelled... what...!!!??

I was already 15 days admitted in the hospital and had now new tests on Monday, I was told that I had two blood clots one in each leg and would need a new treatment for at least another 15 days, I spoke by phone with Carolina early Tuesday, she was just leaving the hotel where she was staying, to walk to the hospital, which was only ten minutes away, walking.

In the next few minutes I read online that a high percentage of cases with a blood clot in the lung, die in the first two hours, another large number of patients die in the first 24 hours? within a few minutes, I felt I lack of air and the doctor, whom was very close, confirmed the result, I had another blood clot in the lung, the situation is very serious, with a high risk of death he said, I could not contain myself and I cried... I was immediately taken to the intensive care area of the hospital, with oxygen and the usual monitoring, Carolina arrived and found my hospital room locked and Simon...??? Where is Simon ??, he chief nurse Mary, explained that for my better care, I had been taken to the intensive care unit, but ten minutes ago...I just talked to him on the phone, Carolina said,... yes, but now he is receiving greater care.

As soon as we saw each other, we just cried and aid how much we loved each other as we were saying that, it all seemed like a nightmare, the events were following too fast... but that was the real situation, medical results and lack of air, oxygen mask, serum, anti-inflammatories, morphine ....there was nothing we could do, but to leave everything in the hands of those who know, the doctors told him to Carolina they were doing everything possible, actually I was in the hands of the Boss, who runs the universe and our destiny, God. Carolina knew very clearly, we have a Chief who decides everything and only he decides, she prayed a lot, without surrendering, Simon??? Do you remember him too?, now you remember him??? is it that you never learn ...???

We phoned Mary of "healing" group and she told us that the message she received, was that I had been "asked for" and was very close to dying, right, it was true, I needed to once again be so close to the end of this earthly life, on the edge death, to remember him, to acknowledge that I had again put idolatry in my daily life, above our Boss, over what I knew was most important, to make sure that I had the ticket for eternity ... !!! ! Maria told Carolina that in fact, my life had been "requested" and would be extremely difficult for me to survive, perhaps the only thing that would save me, would be if she prayed for me and my ancestors for 21 days, Maria gave all the indications of how Carolina should pray and sure enough, on the 21st day, I got a marked improvement on my health...sure enough, we do not help only those around us, our acquaintances, but should also help those that have died before us, pray for them, for the sick, the prisoners, for those who have no one, the results can be seen, they can be felt and cause satisfaction. I spent two days in intensive care and received treatment to prevent blood from clotting, making sure I would not have a lack of oxygen, I was doped, drugged, appreciating every moment of life. Simon, whom do you remember? your youth?, your work ?, the closest people around you? ... And the others?, Simon, in those remarkable moments in your life, do you remember the most at need ?, or you go back to your selfishness and idolatry and worry only about yourself?

it is true, in those moments that you seem to be so near the end, are moments in which one is closer to others and actually easier to anonymously help those who need help, share any suffering of this life. You have so many good people around you, doctors, nurses, cleaning staff, kitchen workers, all do a little to help your physical improvement and many more people in your environment, there are people that may be at great distances, who love you and pray for you, they ask the Boss for help and for you to improve, to get better ...Simon please help...

Feeling such physical weakness of the body, makes you appreciate more your physical health, you want so badly to recover, to get better, it's really so easy to ask the Chief, to help someone else at the same time, the Chief always listens, just ask ... Simon ... Simon ... do you see how easy it is?, do you always need to be reminded and do it the hard way...???

Yet another medical treatment with anticoagulant drugs to prevent new clots from forming, they could be fatal, because a clot can close the passage of blood in a vein and just one dies. You have not finished writing the book I asked you to write, you have not finished explaining your experiences, do it very clearly Simon, so that everyone can understand the messages that you have been given to explain ... ohhh!! how hard it is for you to understand! !! And they are things so simple...!!!

You received a "call" not by phone or by email, but by your "intuition", the same that made you respond "Yes I'm here" when you heard the question "Is there any-

one else there?" being shouted. Don't you think it was an angel again that cares and is very close to you...?
It was a "need" you felt suddenly to call for a Father of the Catholic religion, so that you could talk with you in the hospital. You expressed your "concern" for your mother who was being treated in an "old people's home" in another South American Country, an institution run by nuns.

The Priest gave you a blessing, using the anointing oil, used for the sick. True, I really had that "need" and "concern", but great was my surprise, it was amazing, when two days later I found out that at the same time I received the blessing with that oil, a nurse entered my mother's room in the "nursing home", she was looking for another nurse and thought she had found her, standing next to the bed where my mother was resting quietly, watching, taking care.

The nurse said that the lady was standing fully dressed in white and some grey hair showing, but it was not a nurse, not a person, it was "supernatural", the nurse literally ran away, closed the door and was frightened. I was relieved of the signal indicating that my prayers had been answered, for me it was an angel who had been sent to see my mother, she was being well cared for and accompanied. I have not heard or thought of another explanation for that image of the woman dressed in white, like a human reality, without being an actual human being... My concern could return at any time, if my mother dies, as it became impossible, have all these ailments, it became impossible for me to fly for some time, but I was more comfortable knowing that her soul (the soul of my mother) was ready to enter into eternal life, when ?, that's not my decision, it is a certainty that she will leave someday, like all of us.

You got the "discharge" from the hospital, unable to walk, you came out in a wheelchair, with severe pain on both legs, after being 45 days in the hospital. You are happy to have survived another life-threatening situation? A friend whom is a doctor, said you really had been extremely "lucky", because a lot of cases similar to yours, end up dead very soon and you Simon, you went through all that and are now virtually unscathed, almost normal...!!!. I remember the stages of my life, since I was young was very slim, agile, I liked the sea and to swim, had travelled a lot and usually travelled with a good climate, sunshine and meeting good people, people who always deserved all the best, good friends and family around.

I remembered those days with long shoulder length hair, sun tanned, very healthy, which was the only thing that failed me was my sight and I wore glasses, but now, a few kilos heavier, with little hair, I had not realized that I had travelled many miles in life...

Simon do you pray?, pray in the morning, pray in the evening, pray at night?... regardless of the time, do you fall asleep or get distracted ?, don't think you're the only one... Tell me Simon, when you pray, do you keep in your thoughts images from the Sacred Scriptures?, or maybe im-ages of your loved ones, or perhaps those who have hurt you? or do you keep your mind "blank"?, Have you seen the tubes of oil paint used by painters? They open, use them, close them, they take care of them, so Simon, open them, use them and care for them. What is the point in having the Sacred Scriptures if you don't read them ? use them and care for them", deep from your mind or deep down from your inner self you open your heart, use your mind and care for yourself?

I would say Simon, there's something missing, some-thing is not right, then right away, 5 days later, you were back in the hospital with pain in your legs, shortness of breath and now with pneumonia, short-ness of breath and blood secretions? Already you are well-known person in the hospital, and you Simon, do you remember all those that worked hard trying to improve your physical health?

Simon are very lucky, many people love you, a lot of people keep praying for you and they create an im-pressive "barrier", impenetrable, to protect you from evil, you have a very hard job ahead, you have to make that this protection cover many other people, you have to help others to feel protected and loved, share your luck with others and you will have the tick-et to eternal life guaranteed.

Once again you are learning to walk, do you remember when you walked with crutches and you learned to walk when you were younger?, and then, when you could almost not walk because of the pain in your stomach? look at how lucky you are, again you are learning to walk, walk right and in the right path !!! Do you understand Simon?????...

This is scary!!! ... get on a plane for a 10 hour flight ... !! I feel my blood warming up ... it feels as if it would be boiling inside... !!!, lack of oxygen, keeping calm, breathe deep, better... Carolina told me, but then another flight, 10 hours more...!!! My blood is still feeling "warm" and continue to feel short of breath, wheelchairs at the airports, and then several days to recover, the improvement is amazingly rapid and impressive.

Simon, you are very lucky, you got better incredibly fast, "we will study the images of the tests that have been done to you, to see if what those doctors said, is really what you had" ... another doctor said: "How could you have been so well, then so bad and then so fast, so well again?" ahhh I remember what your travel companion said the other day: "I have seen other similar cases ... especially in the jungle, there is black magic there... and other weird stuff... Simon, do you realize...? You see that your God loves you very much, he shows you the work of the devil and then displays his powers, do you know why he shows you all this...???

Well, try to return to normal life, after seven weeks of "rest" (inactivity), to travel again by plane, repeat old experiences with a different taste, now with a certain difficulty to breathe inside the plane, really a fear of not being able to breathe freely or to be left without any air have gone, the shock of the severe pain in the legs returning, another blood clot... ufff...!! never again...!!!

Tiredness, non-stop activities, wanted to visit my mother, since the doctors said that there was no medical reason to explain why she was still alive, she had lung deficiency, kidney failure, heart failure, it seemed that she was just waiting for something or someone... I got to visit her Friday, Saturday and Sunday, and on Monday I had to travel by plane again, one hour after take-off, my mother passed away, it is as if she had been waiting to see me, flying to her homeland, what a coincidence!!! ...I took the next flight back to her wake and burial. In her last few days, she was very thin and did not speak, could not feed herself, barely moving her eyes, I felt her hand, it was time for the departure of her soul, it was the end of the journey of her body, almost 98 years existence finally old age caught up with her!!! What happiness, her soul has already gone, she managed to get there!!!

Happiness, yes, could I dance?, after being with such serious leg problems ?, Well, five hours dancing made it clear that my work here continues...

The facts are clear to me, that we actually participated in the struggle between "good and evil", we are part of it, just keeping an "normal" life above average between good and evil, we ensure entry to the good side of eternal life... ahh that does not mean for example, that a prostitute sees five clients and then she sees another six for free, she has done more good than bad...!!! The issue is much more complex, but the "idea" is clear.

I never tire of telling you Simon, your mother cared for you to have a healthy birth and to give you the best opportunities in life with your birth. When you die, you will have had a similar opportunity to have done everything necessary, so that your soul has that ticket that allows your soul peace and tranquillity in your eternal life. You eat when you are hungry, you work and you get your salary for you to buy what you need for your comfort in earthly life, sharing with others, do the same to feed your soul with goodness, with peace, with love. Trust me, it is in your interest...

Simon... (silence)... Simon?... (silence)... Simon???...ahhhh... you understood and you achieved it!!!!... Simon you are welcome!!!

About The Author

Simon Kent (also known as Clark Templar) was born when his Chilean parents were living in Lima, Peru in 1953. He studied in the United Kingdom and he entertained himself in Europe and later in Argentina, Chile, Colombia, Brazil, the Caribbean and a few other Countries, where he met people of varied origins and customs. Real stories of journeys by bus, car, aeroplane and even UFO.

He had an ordinary life until unexpectedly, survived a tragic accident on an underground train 30 metres under the ground in the City of London at Moorgate station. It was then that he had a vision of eternity and survived to describe it!

A lover of beaches and beautiful things, tasty and joyful (including his wife Caroline). Now a prominent businessman in Europe and Latin America. He tells of a real life testimony, with anecdotes, about the origin of life and the afterlife, before being born and after death, of this world and of the others (whether present or future), making sure to get the "ticket to eternity", one of the few that has used the return portion of that ticket, including unusual visits and to the two eternal destinations .and survived to tell the story!!!

It has been extremely difficult to write parts of these stories and to have to read them again and correct them, each time crying with emotion, because of the crudeness, ethically incorrect and repugnant of some of the events.

Contents

Dedication
Prologue
Introduction

FIRST PART   **13**
1 The Origins In South America   15
2 Getting to Know Europe   17
3 The Trip To Greece   21
4 Early Moral Ideas   27
5 Carolina Came Into My Life   31
6 The Landslide – Survive   35
7 Karen In Scotland   39
8 Claire In Manchester – Gas, National Priority   45
9 The Sudden Death   49
10 The Ticket To…Eternity   53
11 Is There Anybody Else There???   63

SECOND PART   **81**
12 After Moorgate   83
13 The New South America For Investment   85
14 Carlos The Jackal | 93
15 Astral Travel – The Abduction   95
16 The Flights From New York   101
17 And The Fire At The Hotel?   103
18 Life In Brazil   107
19 Karen And Alberto Passed Away   119
20 Nalda   121
21 Illnesses, Cancer….   125
22 The Pure Energy   129
23 More Signals   133

24 The Continuity Of Life...The Ticket To Eternity...	141
25 Parapraxes	151
26 The roasted meat	157
27 The ceiling collapsed in the London office	161
28 Healing	169
About the Author	183